Fuctifino!

Mandy Ann Brewster

I have often heard: "Its a big club and you ain't in it" said when speaking of the ruling elite (courtesy of George Carling) Which is true but, we have the possibility of joining an infinitely bigger club called "caring humanity" and not many of us are fully paid up members of that either!

Copyright © 2015 Mandy Ann Brewster

All rights reserved.

ISBN-10:1506156487
ISBN-13: 978-1506156484

CONTENTS

	Acknowledgements	i
1	A new beginning	1
2	Positive beliefs	15
3	The negative roots	28
4	Boys will be boys	39
5	Covered in skin	52
6	When two worlds collide	75
7	Seeking transcendence	92
8	Fuctifino	112
9	So f*cking what	128
10	Matriarchy?	143
11	Discovering the planetary script	155
12	A different wrinkle in time	171
13	Red for go!	198

ACKNOWLEDGMENTS

To all the beautiful souls who agreed to act as total a**holes on my journey of discovery:

This one's for you

1 A NEW BEGINNING

Well! A lot has happened since I busted my book writing block, I have discovered so much more about myself. My perspective on my own capabilities has changed. I am also still all the things I always was, just still developing mastery or rather developing my ability to command my own ship, as ever…

If you have not read my first book, it might be an idea to do that before reading further to connect the background info, you on the other hand might just be meant to start here. These books are intended to be a gradual unfolding of my understanding and points worth considering perhaps even for us all in this momentarily fast paced evolution of our race. I am just sharing my journey, knowledge and experiences and whilst people always tell me that they "put what I say to their own experiences", these books are really just my own desire to explain myself and what I have discovered and get it written down with meaning, give my experiences purpose and add my voice to the growing number of people who are trying to raise awareness. If it speaks to you of your experiences, that is great, it means I am not alone ☺

I have struggled with that one all of my life! People always thinking I am talking about them when I am talking about me… It made me feel quite alone for a while as I told my story and people often responded with "So what you are saying is that I or we do this for that reason" etc, etc, etc… I used to want to rid this dynamic from my life, got the hump with people over it at times, and have exclaimed once or twice: "Why the f*ck is it always about you? Why can I never be talking about me"!

Anyway, since qualifying as and becoming a teacher and counsellor, I have found it is a very good gift indeed, even if a trifle lonely at times. But I certainly do not want to get rid of it now I can tell you…

An example of this was when talking to people that had read my first book, a thing that came up a couple of times was; "How can you blame all illnesses on your thinking? Are you are saying it's my fault, or their fault". This took me by surprise as I wasn't aware that I had? I had to go back and check though because I hadn't read it through the eyes of somebody who has had, or still has, a connection to an emotive point in that area. Such as children born with illnesses and people with genetic conditions. I still couldn't spot where I had said that, except maybe in my reference to Louise Hay's list of thinking patterns and illnesses so quite obviously a sore point for them I suppose?

"I get it"! I reckon I might have been the same if I had been lumped with a debilitating or life threatening condition at birth, whether through genetics or otherwise! It might push my buttons too and I might have drawn the same conclusion.

So it was a good point for me to reconsider, it had been

a long time since I delved a bit deeper into the subject of illnesses and thinking connections. Right at my moment of pondering how to start this book, I got an email newsletter from a very brave spiritual astrologer, who has been a source of much support of my understanding of self and is indeed responsible for opening my eyes to the bodhisattva energy and a very significant part of my own jigsaw. This newsletter spoke of her own struggles with illness and so, as she has done before, she unblocked my path.

She wrote so eloquently about her acceptance of her own debilitating condition and her reason for being, that my heart swells with pride to have contact with such a special soul and to know that humans are capable of such greatness.

So I feel that to go deeper into affirmations and what they mean in the first chapter (which is part of my intention for how these books will unfold), it seemed like a good idea and a sign to approach it from the physical condition perspective.

[i]Blessings Sarah-Jane

Thinking = illness is often labeled as "Victim blaming" <u>Lots</u> of people might exclaim; "you are telling me it's my fault"! Like I said, I totally get that perception.

I do however think that is a very inaccurate statement though, as I believe it is, as always, the fault of the environment. Whether through all of the heavy metals and pollutants that are in our goldfish bowl, or the impacts of group think! Or self think; Or genetic pick up, or all of it! None of us are free from the impacts of the environment.

And then I think about the 'fact' That glaucoma is in my family and so is arthritis and they are both considered hereditary so therefore genetic. I do not have glaucoma, even though it is rife in my family history. My mother and my sister both have it. I can't help thinking about the fact that my father was in hospital whilst my mother carried me and that might have something to do with it...

Louise Hay, reckons it means:

"Stony unforgiveness, pressure from long standing hurts, overwhelmed by it all".

Now! That is in my family ancestry I can tell you. On different levels for different people either the recipient of the stony unforgiveness or the perpetrator. I felt it too, but I never got overwhelmed in that though. They never really accepted me into the family did they?

I did have the beginnings of arthritis in my knees though and the swelling of my knees gave me pain. I slept with a pillow between them and often winced in pain climbing stairs or when they knocked together.

Louise Hay says:

Arthritis; Feeling unloved, criticism, resentment

and

Knees; stubborn ego and pride, inability to bend.

That's what the book say's ☺

Well for those of you that don't know me that well, I first of all said; "that's crap"!

Then because I am a Gemini and my energy moves fast, immediately accepted it, because I saw it in me and started to criticize myself for having had too much pride and was absolutely "adamant" That I had let myself down. No wonder nobody loved me!

Hahaha! There it all was! All in that first statement!

[ii]I had also been recently investigating Andrew Norton-Webber and the distilled water knowledge. So as always, I had decided to try it out for myself before making any judgments. Of course only after lots of research of my own on positive/negative attraction, the difference between organic and inorganic minerals, ancient practices and water molecule structure etc.

I was trying this at the time (Still do only drink distilled water if I can) and also started saying affirmations based on my exploration of my past childhood "pick up points" and rewriting the meaning... My knees are now better! Thanks to the distilled water and the thought grappling, exploration and then change in perception and diet of course. Well I get a little issue with them every now and again, but it's always linked to times when I am judging myself for being "proud" and not eating very well or drinking distilled water enough etc.... These are after all; historically embedded principles and beliefs that are very apparent in my "genetic beliefs ancestry" so therefore are going to be harder to shift. There is as much if not more evidence for this holding true as there is for the "biological genetic <u>theory</u>" it is after all just a "theory" and not many people know that. Mainly because they haven't researched it and also because of the way it is presented as scientific fact!

Our eating habits, beliefs and values are also all passed down generationally, they become part of the water in the "fish bowl" that we call our "culture" and as highlighted in the first book, we do not notice until we are taken out of it. There is a spiritual theory, and some cultures would call it fact, that a child born with a life threatening genetic illness, has come to bring a very special message. Not only to the family that they were born into but also to the world. In effect, this would make them very special souls indeed. Think about it, they are grappling with the beliefs of major amounts of people in the society they are in. Not only the beliefs that could be connected to the illness that are rife in society and the collective unconscious, but also the major belief in it not being curable! Then any of their own beliefs that might be lurking somewhere in their unconscious, Jesus Christ! Did they choose a task? And if this is indeed what is playing out, then they, my friends, are true saints and very brave souls indeed!

Of course on the other hand there is still the theory that

we are just a victim of our genes and therefore just a biological accident, where you were the unlucky one and can do nothing about it, that's it! As always, if this is your understanding, I would advise that you investigate it further. No point in standing up for a belief if you can't present evidence of why that is so, just your own belief and experiences. You might even discover that the "genetic biological inheritance theory" all stems from a central "dogma" yep that's right; a belief. Not a scientific fact but a belief!

Perhaps that belief might be so? You can believe what you like, because after all, it is just a belief. But for me, I like the other idea, it's more empowering, makes more sense and have gathered enough evidence to satisfy me through trial, error and investigation at this point to really connect it to my present beliefs. It really is an individual journey and you are entitled to believe what bit of it you like. You might even believe the dark thing that genetic illness is about punishment and bad karma. I must admit I do not like that theory one bit, so I ain't buying it; and it is also a form of victim blaming! Whatever your belief, you would be wise to investigate it yourself though to highlight your own understanding, even if you do resonate with it and think it is correct, you might eventually uncover the truth…

A for instance of how this plays out is; sickle cell disease, which is a genetically passed on severe anaemic condition that affects only certain races. I find it a connection worthy of note, that in Louise Hay's list it is connected to "A belief that one is not good enough, which destroys the very joy of life" and the fact that there has been genocide in the relatively recent genetic memory of these same people and actually still is. Racism is still very much alive and kicking across our planet, (This system could not survive without it) and as is evident, we pass things on generationally through our insistence that our children are empty vessels which we must fill with our knowledge and experience.

There are of course some possible connections to sickle cell trait and the resistance to malaria so also some interesting parallels with evolution and the metaphysical cause being listed as "out of synch with nature"! The development of malaria was apparently linked to deforestation and the "trait" appeared at the same time to create immunity. This could possibly have developed in destructive ways once the oppression got more intense and turn into full blown sickle cell anaemia. It is of course just an idea but it sounds like it could be linked to the spread of patriarchy and masculine value dominance.

It may be that the family that you come from are absolutely different to this! It may be that they were indeed great and noble spiritual warriors, but it is also worthy of note that "nothing exists in a vacuum" We are all on this planet and we all get impacted in some ways, however different our experiences might be. The environment and the collective (un)conscious could well be the key here. Anyway, like I said, none of us are right if we reject others view-points and experiences. We are all holding pieces of the jigsaw and whatever your belief, your soul agenda is behind it somewhere. We all have our paths to follow! I try very hard not to get into one track ideologies and I often don't succeed because it is impossible, the whole bloody thing is just an idea you see! I am however just trying to share "my discoveries" I am sure there are lots of others and I really do hope I still have much to learn.

[iii]Bruce Lipton has done some great stuff on "epigenetics" really fascinating and mind bending in its simplicity "the biology of belief". You might want to check it out further…

Anyway; this is how the epigenetics theory goes, put even more simply "Mandy style" ☺

The environment is responsible for the genetic creation and growth of what cells eventually become. In a pregnancy this goes like this; Information from outside the cell creates the baby inside the womb. The information comes from the perception of what the mother thinks the developing child will need to become for its survival and the evolution of our species, they also pass on impacts.

Check it out; Bruce Lipton knows more about this piece of the jigsaw than yours truly, he is after all a "stem cell" scientist!

So in effect, the environment on planet Earth, which at this time, has been created by the imbalance of power and masculine values, is ultimately responsible for all of it...

How can this be victim blaming?

What about if the people who asked me the question stopped reading at that point? In the "real" world, our own beliefs and values could be creating a block to discovering the rest of the story, but does your soul need to know this at this time for your own pathway to unfold?

I know I have often thrown a book away in disgust because it said something that I disagreed with, only to pick it up later (I try not to do this too often), although some of these were kind of merited. Like one book I read that said we were all affected by the desire to have sex with our opposite parent at around the age of 3 to 6. This theory was the work of Freud and is called the Oedipus complex. This grew from the remnants of his "seduction" theory, where he decided that his patients had not been sexually abused but "wished they had" ☹ He also blamed women for pretty much everything and said that boys developed a fear of castration and girls got jealous of boy's penises SHEESH! To me these theories are extremely flawed and indeed have been largely discredited. So really not an ideology I wanted to buy into! Although the developing understanding of Psychodynamic counseling theory was accredited to Freud, the bits that actually hold water and are relevant in the general population are nothing to do with Freud's fantasies! Especially the one about women as non-creative except biologically so! But they do play out in our subconscious programming. Thanks Freud! I also discovered that he connected creativity to the unconscious and found out he had said that because women have smaller super egos than men, they rely, he said, on their unconscious rather than their conscious to drive them through life. He also said that this makes them hysterical and of course as a consequence this would mean not suitable for cool headed leadership! WTF ! Not only did we have sexism here but also a huge contradiction within that sexist belief!

I wanted to rip that "Mother f**ker"[iv] to shreds I can tell you!

Nawal El Saadawi the amazingly brave Egyptian feminist writer/speaker/doctor wrote very well in her paper on "Women, Creativity & Mental Health" in 2001, about how this theory impacted within all of the other ideologies that women on this planet experience, and are still impacted on to this very day...

I didn't give much credence to what these masculine, white middle class theorists said about human behavior than I had to after that, other than to argue against the crazy points. Not until much, much later at least, once I had realized that they were giving us insight into how "elitist" or "privileged" minds work! I got into that as my journey unfolded.

For instance In Freud's paper "Totem and taboo" it is very clear to see that he assumes indigenous people were "primitive" and because they had a "civilization" different to his own patriarchal view of what that means, decided they were at the "beginning" of their development. He believed that the developmental patterns of the psyche were responsible for shaping civilization and we could learn much about the "unconscious" from a people that he had quite obviously decided had little or no consciousness operating mainly from the unconscious. In other words "of low intelligence" and in their evolutionary beginnings.

So you see! It is a block creator or a block buster when we throw something away just because we disagreed with something that was either said or we misinterpreted. We miss something! But as always, when the student is ready, the teacher appears. I wasn't ready at that point to use the information from this fully but it did serve as a wake-up call at that time to question everything.

All of it is important; it just needs to be at the right time...

A very negative environment it is for sure! Especially when you consider the amount of power those leaders or rather, those who control the money that are role-playing their privileged and entitled parts have over our "normality" or in other words, our "Goldfish bowl water".

Freud's nephew Edward Bernays took all this crap ideology to America. Yes, without a doubt he understood the impact of the subconscious and it's ability to manipulate people's opinions and desires, but the underlying beliefs about "people" were just a projection of a white, middle class, masculine ideology passed down from a small percentage of powerful people who pull the strings. A masculine ideology that a few centuries earlier had done the very same thing and infected the same environment through other means. This time though, the ideology was far wider reaching. It didn't stop at the indigenous populations, it led to a speeding up of world dominance! It was in fact an ideology driven by an "elitist" and hierarchical mind-set. A famous quote by Edward Bernays sums this up:

"The conscious and intelligent manipulation of the organized habits and opinions of the masses is an important element in democratic society. Those who manipulate this unseen mechanism of society constitute an invisible government which is the true ruling power of our country. ...We are governed, our minds are molded, our tastes formed, our ideas suggested, largely by men we have never heard of. This is a logical result of the way in which our democratic society is organized. Vast numbers of human beings must cooperate in this manner if they are to live together as a smoothly functioning society. ...In almost every act of our daily lives, whether in the sphere of politics or business, in our social conduct or our ethical thinking, we are dominated by the relatively small number of persons...who understand the mental processes and social patterns of the masses. It is they who pull the wires which control the public mind."

Perhaps it could be used as a recipe to rule the world AKA The capitalist system? If you want to do that, and I am not suggesting it is being done on purpose (but it might be) you first gotta infiltrate the subconscious ideology and develop the bits that suit the "Man" by bombarding people with symbolism and subtle innuendo of what they must become to be "good enough" and what might happen to them if they don't... Always present them with an image of the "greatness" of the leaders and their ideology. Isolate them from other perspectives or even ridicule those perspectives even state that they are "evil". Then tell them how inferior they are because of; gender, culture, skin color, belief systems, class, behavior etc and there we have it. The reason we follow the "ones at the top" We have been formed in the image of these invisible men!

Now that sounds a bit familiar doesn't it!

World domination could realistically come from this very principle and the media become the tap that drips the polluted water steadily into the goldfish bowl and creates all the crap from which we grow. Is it any wonder that we get ill or are born with so called genetic illnesses?

Somebody once said to me; "We all have two washing machines, one for our clothes and the other one for our brains. It took me a while to work out she was talking about the TV ☺

2 POSITIVE BELIEFS

The patriarchal hierarchy is structured in such a way that it forms a kind of pyramid where the power and wealth is all at the top and shared among a very few, the closer to the bottom the lesser the power and wealth and the more of us there are. It seems clear to me that we need to start making changes from the bottom up! The bottom of the pyramid does after all, hold up the top.

Yes, it is a truism that the ones at the top have all the power, but that is also just because we believe it is so! Just think for a moment what it would be like and what would happen, if everybody except the ones that are pulling the strings in this system, just suddenly said NO! We ain't doing that anymore! How would they enforce the system then? Send in the army? Nobody, except perhaps the ones pulling the strings in the military wins in this system. The same with the police force, the prison service, the legal system, the financial system etc. Everybody else, even those closest to the top would benefit from system change. That would just leave a very minor amount of people who do already 'benefit' (and even that benefit is arguable) trying to enforce a genocidal system on billions with no military, financial or legal strength whatsoever! That just wouldn't happen would it? We might all just tell them to go get stuffed!

Neither would the idea that "everybody" wakes up at once and says NO Happen either! Well, I don't think so anyway. It would be interesting if it did, and my greatest idealistic beliefs, drive me forward to consider this every day. But with my present knowledge of the human race and the process of change, I doubt very much that this is probable and I am not so sure that would be a good idea anyway... Think about it! Even if it did happen, what about all the patterns of behavior, beliefs and values that are embedded in our collective unconscious? What about all of our "in-fighting"? What about our trust issues? How long would it take before our past experiences began to warp our view of our fellow humans? How soon before we start projecting? And we are always attracting anyway! How soon before the parallel processes start to play out? How soon in fact would it be before we created another system the same or more intense?

History is littered with events of popular uprisings and revolutions, even escapes to "brave new worlds" like America and Australia and nothing much has changed for around 7 thousand years, except that the pyramid got reinforced and the same patriarchal culture became normalized. Think about it, violent or even non-violent revolution, where governments are thrown out, relies heavily on masculine energy to succeed. These are always led by masculine principles of "force" be it violent or peaceful... Without balancing the feminine side (acceptance), that masculine force will once again dominate. Without change in ourselves, system change is impossible, Fact!

 Without most people involved balancing the feminine with the masculine and getting the "f**k out" of our unbalanced value system of self importance, divide and rule consciousness and blame of others, then this negative imbalance of masculine energy will once again rise and turn into a pyramid.

We can however start to make the changes needed in ourselves to accomplish a more balanced eventuality, instantly!

Let's look at what positive thinking means. In my early days of affirmations, my first consideration for manifestation, involved "getting on in the world" Getting a car, a better house, a great job. I was just so very lucky that I had gone so far down the pan that I had also been forced to look at my "unworthiness" in detail and so had been also manifesting forgiveness of self and others. But basically, I had been focusing on possessions and status, a capitalist dream! I understand how alluring possessions and status are from the viewpoint of one who had "nothing" and was "nobody" ... To be given a tool to create whatever I wanted was like being a kid in a sweet shop! I loved the idea of the "cosmic kitchen" cooking up all my orders. I had found a book called [v]"The secret" which explained the process and also introduced me to the world of "atoms" and quantum physics. This book was quite heavily focused on "getting more", "becoming more". It was kind of a reflection/product of the system in that, to gain people's attention within capitalist ideology, you need to be offering those things. But it was also a very good way of helping people to become more aware of the magic of spirituality. I dabbled a bit with the manifestation of wealth thing, but it didn't work for me. I remember I once wrote out a great big cheque (In size rather than amount) and pinned it on my bedroom door, so that it was the first thing I saw when I woke up and last thing when I went to bed. I laugh now, because it was so obvious that my prosperity consciousness was pretty poor when I wrote that cheque, it was for £250.00 ☺

It was all I felt I was worth; consequently I couldn't even manifest that!

This book was invaluable in my development though, I discovered quantum physics and the science of energy and creation..

It impacted well on the other stuff like, developing positive self beliefs and curing my addictions, achieving my goals, understanding myself etc but money and wealth manifestation was beyond me. I only wanted enough to stop me worrying about losing my home every time I thought about paying my rent! I didn't want any more than that, but my god I struggled with this; still do sometimes.

I didn't care much for world peace in those days either, I just thought that I could help others not to become "piss-heads" and show them how to get out of the crap and into the wonderful society that awaits them. I was going to write a book and become a counselor. I was going to stay on benefits and counsel people for nothing. I never gave it a thought that I could earn a living at it. So it is not surprising that my physical manifestation of wealth was always and still is somewhat stunted. I do after all if you remember from the first book, have very little need to be rich and no desire whatsoever to do anything unless it floats my boat!

The point I am making here is that even though I was less affected by the desire to have "things" than lots of people are, I still started my spiritual journey with a list of what I wanted to own and to be. I gave very little thought to the impact that world peace might have and when I did, it was always about what others needed to do. I liked the idea though but we were not at war in England were we? It's the other countries that have got to sort that out isn't it? Nothing whatsoever to do with me, we are at peace in this country; I thought!

I knew nothing about how the [vi]capitalist system works; I knew nothing about how our country is only affluent because we are accumulating and controlling all the resources of others in faraway lands. Not just England but the west. I was not aware that my relatively "cushy" lifestyle was built on the back of poverty and destruction across the world. I was not aware that all the resources were being siphoned off; upwards of course, towards the top.

You know what they say... If you want to find the cause of the problem; follow the big money!

At this time I truly believed that If I didn't "duck and dive" anymore, I would be instructing the universe that I could get a living and survive in other ways now. I would be accepted into this peaceful and wonderful society if I lived as if I already was it, then I would get it or become it. I really believed that if I loved my bills then I would get the money to pay them. The problem was, there were just so many of them to love and they just kept growing!

I just couldn't get my arms around them all, or myself out of the fear of no money. Mainly because I didn't have a pot to p*ss in!

During my university years this intensified. My student loan went mainly on paying my rent. I had 3 hours a week paid teaching work and was doing a full day a week voluntary counseling and running a domestic abuse program, and three hours a week working on a woman's reconnection course I had developed for which I got paid. Saturday morning saw me running a drop-in centre for people with mental health sickness. This filled every moment of my life as I struggled to cope with the demands of this whilst studying two full time university courses and developing my recovery from substance abuse at the same time. The courses I was on to gain these qualifications absolutely demanded this too.

A super human fete indeed!

As my struggle with money was very much connected to my father's beliefs about me (first book) I had been traumatically conditioned to not attract money, the fact that this turned out to be the best way for me is great but not really "self" helpful when considering how this version of the world works.

I think about how this works the other way too, imagine being born into a family that reiterates your importance and special deservedness. You are also told that you are better than others and are entitled to your very special position and your wealth. On top of this you are taught that you have a superior way of life and others are there to serve and adore you and of course, strive to be like you. Consider how that also might be in reality? How much of having and doing anything you want at the expense of others, might you be able to deal with? Would it not get a bit mundane? Or crazy even? Just like it always does, whatever level you reach in addictions. Where would you seek excitement from if you had already done it all or could do whatever you wanted? This to me is a very loaded question indeed and one that I have often grappled with over the years...

A little bit like my own semi-addiction to chocolate. When I am not in possession of sweets or chocolate and the fancy overcomes me, I have got to undertake a "mission" to get some. It might not be much of a mission, like getting dressed and walking to the corner shop, but it's still a mission. The desire usually only overtakes me when I have become bored. I get to the shop and I buy so much bloody chocolate and sweets that I really don't fancy any of it when I get home. I am spoilt for choice. When I have chocolate I don't want it. In fact it makes me feel sick! I don't even mind other people eating it all. Abundance absolutely enhances my gift giving capabilities; I only hoard 'sometimes' when resources are scarce and even then not very successfully. I can usually be persuaded with very little effort to part with my last possession.

But what about if I had a huge sense of entitlement, and possessed most of the resources? Coupled with a belief that others do not deserve it by accident of birth family and must work for everything I give them? Or they must at least give me something in exchange that's worth more. Add an absolute addiction to, or dependence on, the "buzz" of total power that needs to be fed. Then what about if I vehemently blamed the skint ones for their position of birth and their behaviors that are caused by their lack of resources? Believed that unless I controlled them, they would make pigs of themselves? Maybe even kill each other or me! How might I act then? Then also how also might the lack of resources and scarcity enhance the desire for the thing that I control?

If I can't have chocolate Man do I want it!

I remember as a young teenager in Holloway prison I became fixated on a certain chocolate bar "Golden cup" I don't think you can get them now. You certainly couldn't get them in there! It was a little slim, thin chocolate bar filled with caramel and rounded at the end, finished off with a smooth golden foil wrapper. It just became so big in my list of desires, so big in fact, that the only thing I wanted to do when I got out of there was buy one and eat it! For three long weeks I fantasized chocolate wrapped in gold!

I had just been collected upon my release by a friend of the bloke I had taken the blame for (The future father of my 5 children) and subsequently had ended up inside for 3 weeks as a consequence of my bloody naiveté! I immediately felt rejected and not good enough because he was not there. He had actually been arrested for something else he had done and was in prison himself. I also found out that he had sold the caravan we were living in with all my possessions in it. I believed I was pregnant, was in fact and had just been faced with the possibility that he had f**ked off and I had no clothes and no home! But I buried those feelings and continued, single minded, in my pursuit of chocolate! Needless to say, it did not live up to my expectations...

Think about it! what does it take to get to the top and how glittering like gold is that addiction to absolute power? Then where do we get the next "buzz"? Consider this alongside a generationally passed on set of values, beliefs and behaviors, how might somebody play out that role? We need to get some empathy going here, not what you with your generationally passed on beliefs, behaviors and values might do, but what somebody with a generationally passed on sense of superiority and little regard for the masses might do. Remember not to project your sense of humanity gleaned from your struggles on to one who has never struggled! That is called "sympathy" which is a wonderful tool for helping us to love others but never does much to uncover the truth like empathy does.

Remember, these are a little generalized too. I am sure saints and sinners can be found within all classes! Princess Diana for example, appears to be one who understood the struggles of everyday people and came from the upper echelons of society.

Addictions absolutely control our behaviors. A desire for the "golden cup" helped me ignore the reality of my situation. Heroin addiction can lead people into all sorts of immoral acts to find the money for their next fix. So too can addiction to power and possessions, whether it's hording money and other resources or feeling the buzz of absolute power.

In this context "As above, so below" seems quite telling...

Think about if I was the only heroin dealer. How might I manipulate those addicted to heroin to control them? How might 'favouritizing' some of the addicts, who in turn can 'favouritize' others, lead to "my way" being followed?

In relation to how the capitalist hierarchy is run, If you can get people believing that they must have stuff to be worthy or can get them addicted to it, and you control that stuff, then you can infiltrate even their spiritual journey. The media and advertising will do most of the fooling; your belief in your own entitlement would do the rest, you wouldn't even need to intend it!

It could definitely lead to others making affirmations like:

"I now have a wonderful new car" "I now have a wonderful new man"

Or, they might even write out a giant cheque for £250.00!

Our journey at this present moment is dependent on finding the money to survive. That's how it is! I absolutely detest the fact that I was born into the only species on planet Earth that makes itself pay to be here. If I didn't have the money to pay for my rent, my food, my fuel, my phone and my internet, etc, I would not be able to function and follow my chosen path. Especially considering also my failure at manifesting a wonderful man! ☺

I suppose if I became destitute and somebody noticed me and my abilities among the rest of the homeless forgotten people and pushed me forward, it might not matter so much, but somehow I don't think that's going to happen do you? I also do not want to be rescued thank you very much! I don't object to the odd savior coming along now and again when I am really stuffed, I am eternally grateful, but I don't really like the idea of dependence on others much, not within this system anyway! So I am afraid that even in my highest ideal, my hands are at this moment tied and I still need money, just like you do.

I often said of my teaching, that I would do the job for nothing! Money does not drive this desire. If money disappeared overnight and everything was free, I would still do that job. In fact I would probably do a better one and work harder at it, because if the financial concerns were taken out of the education system, the paperwork would all but disappear, I would be free to create! I did in fact do loads of my teaching paperwork for nothing; lots of teachers spend many hours doing work outside of their paid hours. Trouble is, for me, it led to burnout; within this capitalist system if you work "for the man" with passion you get eaten alive!

You see, the trick, I had discovered, was to work at the thing I am passionate about, throw my heart and soul into it, give it meaning, make it count; whilst trying with all my might and stubbornness to keep out of the fear of money! Then as if by magic, the money always appears. But because we live in a system of power and control, I must now work for myself or once again be eaten alive!

I discovered my process and a hidden conditioned belief that "something always turns up" which came from my very early years of following my heart and not giving much thought for tomorrow or the outcome.

This transition from "working for the man" to "working for myself" might give me a few scary moments with this type of manifestation I can tell you, but I am still here, and I am still on it!

So for me at least, positive affirmations are not helpful if they involve competition or possessions. Consider how much power those at the top have in creating their own wealth and manifesting their hearts desires and then consider what it does to them and ultimately the rest of humanity...

Affirming my abundance means balancing the abundant sources, like forgiveness, finding meaning, my connection to others, my own and others rights to have our physical and comfort needs met and to enjoy the abundance of resources of love and support and beauty that has little to do with possessions. To work in a job that I love, freely and with passion, to be able to live and work in beautiful surroundings. In effect togetherness!

To believe that I am worthy of imparting the wisdom I have gleaned from my journey with meaning, purpose and foresight. To believe that I will find the opportunity to share this with others freely and lovingly and to be welcomed into the human family, is nowadays my most often needed affirmation I can tell you!

To work on this with any depth, not only involves discovering myself, but also my fellow humans and shining a light on what we have collectively created in our past within this once growing and now dissolving pyramid of oppression.

Just following our path and sometimes acting on impulse can pay great dividends...

3 THE NEGATIVE ROOTS

I stumbled across the "freedom fighter" path I am on now, quite by chance. I had been on the spiritual path for well over a year, started my counselor training, moved house and begun my "new life" working towards becoming a "professional". I had a lot of fun in those days, carrying my brief case and wearing "smart" clothes as I went off to my 2nd year course. It was really quite enjoyable, not to be asked for my ticket on the train, not to be treated with suspicion by my fellow humans, to be spoken to politely by "official people" and to be revered in some ways by others. This was of course relative to my past experiences with officialdom and the general public. I had after all just come through 6 years of substance addictions, quite publicly acted out too I might add. Before that I had been treated as "the gypsy woman" or "the woman with the big mouth and loads of kids" etc. Then of course before that, the big mouthed uncontrollable teenager! So you see a vast difference that pretty much went with this new perspective that the world was wonderful.

I was on "probation" in those days, like I said, my addictions had played out publicly and I got myself nicked quite often for "substance induced" offences. There was a time that I was in court at least once a month and sometimes, once a week! I was well known by all the officials in my local magistrate's court and most of the police in the area. I can recall a time when I had conducted my own trial drunk! I quite often laugh about that one, I can be very dramatic at times and I played that one to the full.

"I put it to you my lord, that the police constable is fabricating the evidence, in effect lying" I said, as I posed with one finger pointed towards the sky and another hooked into my waistcoat pocket, whilst allowing a dramatic pause...

I can still remember their stifled grins as I was strutting my stuff, in full glory as the "learned defense barrister" p*ssed of course! ☺

Anyway, to get back to the point; I had the use of the probation office careers advisor and because I was also a "recovering addict", got a lot more help with arranging interviews etc. My careers officer had offered to help me to find a voluntary placement and said he would make some phone calls to arrange this for me. He suggested DGS MIND a mental health charity and said that people are often put off because they are scared of mental health. Well he was right about that one! I was in a real dilemma! "I", remember; was the totally perfect, non-judgmental spiritual being! But; I still did not want to work with a load of "crazy people" though ☹ Oh man! In those days, I had a real problem saying no, and also not wanting to admit, that I was being judgmental, not really realizing just how judgmental I was being actually, not to mention "brain washed", I blurted out; "well really I want to work with domestic abuse".

I wanted to do what? It had not entered my mind before that moment. I didn't want to work with domestic abuse! I just thought, why would I want to help somebody get away from violence, its not really an area I can use my spiritual counseling skills in. I knew this knowledge would not have helped me when I was being knocked around. In fact I knew it might make things worse! But, I was committed now and within a few weeks was working in the local refuge, just 5 minutes walk from my new home.

I was bored witless! My CRB check was taking ages to come through and I was not allowed to be alone with the women until it did. I was relegated to "office duties" cleaning up etc. Occasionally I was allowed to help a woman fill out a form for benefits or housing aid and I detest forms. I can never work out what it is they are asking me. I can see lots of potential meanings to the questions! I would even go so far as to say I have "form phobia"! But there was this course they wanted me to go on called "[vii]Freedom" and I loved it. I could use my newly developing skills and also learn about abuse dynamics. It was a bit of a double edged sword though, because my eyes were opened pretty damned quick I can tell you! I listened and contributed in discussions and was introduced to the reasons why domestic abuse is about power and control and is, I later discovered for myself, a bloody addiction.

I was amazed to find out that my experiences within abuse were pretty much universal. The same tactics were used, the same beliefs, the same type of reasoning and the same trap! I also discovered that I had utilized some of these tactics myself after fleeing the relationship. The abused had become the abuser! I grabbed that one pretty quickly I can tell you. Oh my god I found ways in myself that had disempowered others, which had given me control by taking control. I had a lot of shame and anger as I discovered that abuse was not just violence but also manipulation. It was about power and control and nothing whatsoever to do with the "excuses" given by the perpetrator.

I was dunk! I had a bad childhood! I have mental health issues! I was jealous! I have trust issues! I was under stress! Etc, etc, etc. These are certainly all things that can create difficult feelings for all of us, but what about the ones who suffer them that do not abuse others? You see, controlling somebody else through force or coercion is not about internal struggles. It is about a belief in superiority and that bullying works!

The main adult victims of domestic abuse are women. That doesn't mean that there is no violence or abuse perpetrated against husbands by wives, it just means that male superiority and an environment that supports patriarchy will also support and enforce the sexist beliefs and create the trap that we now call domestic abuse. This patriarchal system supports sexism and men's rights and whatever way you approach it, leads most of us to believe that we need to be ruled. Domestic abuse is only a trap because of the rules and masculine privilege! I would even go so far as to say that the violence, whilst being physically dangerous and devastating maybe even fatal, does not do the damage that emotional and psychological abuse cause to those who survive it. Yes it is the immediate, ultimate fear, but is not the thing that makes you stay or pass it on.

Whilst there are many facets to the in-depth 'psychological' understanding of domestic abuse, they are but a smoke screen that has been created in our struggle to find a cure.

The subject of domestic abuse has been considered and researched extensively over the years resulting in a mass of conflicting data and much misunderstanding and confusion.

During my university years, I read a paper that put "masochism" as the reason women stay in abuse. I had a field day with that one I can tell you!

When we confuse symptoms with causes, we end up with many dynamics and theories that rely on abnormality of behaviors from societal norms to prove other theories are wrong. We then get into arguments as to what is different between symptoms and dynamics which leads us on an 'Alice in wonderland' style journey further away from the discovery of the cause.

With regard to this, put simply; there are differences between men and women and they do mainly take "traditional" roles. "Traditionally" Men are taught that they are the dominant species and Women taught to be subordinate. Although there are many facets to this view and many examples of difference, this is a cultural creation and a norm within all societies.

Devaluing of the woman coupled with narcissistic parallels to governmental relationships with society are the Cause. The pursuit of power on every level is reflected within the abusive relationship! Nobody is to blame, neither man nor woman and we are all victims of this system. We just need to change the view (by whatever means) that women are meant to be subordinate. Stop devaluing a woman's role, and instead realize that the woman in society carries one of the most sacred tasks (among all her other abilities) and that is, creation of life and nurturing the generations that will be in 'command of this ship' after we are gone. She doesn't even have to have actually given birth, she still represents fertility and mothering in all of its guises with her feminine form. Then think about where our value system is! If she doesn't value herself and society doesn't value her greatness, then how on earth are we going to teach this to the next generation and change the environment we are presently surviving in?

Domestic abuse is defined as: any behavior designed to frighten or manipulate the victim with the aim of exerting control over their freedom of choice. This can be physical, mental or emotional and is the most widely accepted definition used when working with this issue.

This topic is important in my work as a counselor/lecturer working with or teaching others about working with victims of domestic abuse as there are potentially huge problems that can be caused by putting the onus on the woman to change, as opposed to helping her to recognize that 'normality' within this society has in some ways indoctrinated her into accepting bad behavior and her lowly status.

Traditionally counseling theory has tended to put the onus of change onto the client, looking at psychological processes within the person and eliciting personal responsibility to change. However the recent success of the 'Freedom program' and findings of the professionals working within this area, have laid the 'blame' firmly on the imbalance of power within relationships.

The Freedom program philosophy states that the sole reason for domestic abuse is 'power and control', with mental health, substance abuse, and childhood experiences being seen as excuses used by the perpetrator to avoid facing up to his responsibility.

The Duluth power and control model asserts that women are the main sufferers. This model emphasizes the gender imbalance when working with domestic abuse because it focuses on the experiences of women within abusive relationships whereby it is noted that;

> *"Male violence against women is a significant problem within society with men responsible for 86-97% of all criminal assaults".* (www.the**duluthmodel**.org)

A power and control wheel[viii] was developed emphasizing a range of abuse tactics used by men against women to exert control (see appendix).

The subject of domestic abuse is often criticized as being biased in support of women and brings up many criticisms whereby feminist views are, some might argue, unfairly seen as anti-male and do not take into account the relatively few cases of abuse by a woman onto a man.

When women use violence in an intimate relationship it has a very different dynamic. Men's use of violence is learned and reinforced by society and women on the other hand do not have the same kind of "back up" from this system. Another point worthy of note is that often women's violence is a response to the controlling violence used against them. There is a vast difference not only caused by the views of what is normal in our society but also quite simply in the general size and strength difference between men and women.

For instance; What do we generally say when a man walks away from his children? If he gives money for their upkeep and sees them once a week etc? What about if a woman leaves the children and does the same? Now you might be a wonderfully enlightened spiritual warrior and truly believe that there should be no more judgment directed at the woman than the man. You would also be deluded if you thought that this was the "normal" response from society.

"How could she leave the kids"! is something I have come across many times when talking in groups and even just in general, yet no such statement has ever been uttered in my presence by man or woman about a man that leaves. Then also, if a woman hits a man, she is largely condemned by both genders and the other way around not much is often heard from men. I have even often heard women say "Yea, he was wrong to hit her, but you don't know what she did to him do you"? Whilst also not hearing much about what the man might have done to the woman if it had been the other way around! I know these are generalizations but I was surprised at the amount of students and clients that shared experiences of themselves or others acting this one out. We women really do keep each other in line! If domestic abuse had been a woman's responsibility, we would have sorted it out years ago!

When we look more deeply into this we can expose the "trap" that is a direct result of our cultural conditioning and show the difference in a gender specific way. Children are the link to discovering an escaped woman's hide out and there are often fatal consequences to this. An example of this happened in a Sheffield refuge. A woman was traced by her partner through the "contact centre" arrangement that had been ordered by our courts who are likely to grant access to fathers unless you can prove beyond doubt that he is violent. This is usually very difficult as most women do not tell anybody about the abuse let alone report these incidents to the police and so therefore often no proof is available. Even fathers who are identified as abusive will still be able to see their children in a contact centre. The father quietly followed the children and their escort back to the Sheffield refuge and blew their mothers head off with a shotgun! You often cannot hide successfully with children unless you go miles away from everybody you know. Even then you will be easily traceable if the person who is trying to find you is persistent or wily enough. Women also believe that he will find them wherever they go. It is an important part of the abusive relationship conditioning.

I was staying in a refuge many years ago and was traced there by my ex telling the police that I was not in my right mind and he thought his children were in danger. The police told him where I was or at least, where the local refuge was. Things have changed since then when it comes to the "rules" around protecting women and this information is not allowed to be given out now, the courts are becoming more aware of this dynamic and it is getting a little bit easier to deny an abusive father access. It is though still a small step, rules very rarely change attitudes and these agencies still think in boxes!

The only way I was able to escape was to leave my children behind, after many attempts in which I had tried to escape with them but ended up going back, for fear of mine and my loved ones safety. If I had not eventually got away, I would have now been dead and he would have been in prison. Unless of course he used the "provocation" route and then he would likely have got off! My guilt and judgment from others would have been a lot worse, if I hadn't got my children back 6 months later.

So you see, the judgment from society and ourselves on what a good mother must do creates a very difficult trap. Plus the reason women judge other women so harshly if they do this, is because we love our children so much that it is unthinkable!

As I am writing this, the Jeremy Kyle show springs to mind, where often single mothers are criticized for not being perfect and a drain on the system. You know, stuff like; "she got herself pregnant to get a council house". On the other hand the resounding applause that is heard when a single father who looks after his children comes on stage is such a stark contrast that you cannot help but see that we generally "think" it is more ok(ish) for a father to leave. You know; "boys will be boys" And all that!

4 BOYS WILL BE BOYS

It was during one "freedom" session that the reality hit home. I had become a bit concerned about the impact of the women on each other and the anger that was coming up towards men in this particular session. It is a very important part of developing a balanced view, that it is reiterated often, that not all men are like this. There is such a thing as a non-abusive man! After all, if women believe that men are "all the same" then the most probable response would be to just "grin and bear it". There are of course examples of the pendulum swinging too far the other way and women turning into man haters. This however is not, contrary to popular belief, the norm!

I had started to lead the discussion in the area of "what a healthy man is like", when a woman said; "the two men I love most on this planet are abusive"! A lot of the women looked at her with surprise and some of them with disgust.

"You see", she said; "They are my sons"...

It was a show stopper! As it clarified an existing belief already present in the women, that actually we are all victims of victims. Whilst we certainly divest all the power in one gender, they are not happy either and are all sons of mothers that love them. Yes, I know there will always be exceptions to the mother love rule, but believe me most if not all of us love our children (and our men) whatever they do. These men were once boys!

The guilt and shameful feelings in the room were tangible...

So what is it that we teach our boys?

Well for a start, the toys are mostly about "masculine" pursuits of power! Guns, soldiers, "he man" stuff, cars and tools and sports equipment etc, no floppy bunnies and dollies for them to look after. What about the washing machines, cookers, Irons? How old were the little boys you know and love, when they stopped playing with them? We also encourage them to be strong and not cry, to be a soldier and a hero! We expect them to play fight and compete; we even sometimes call them things like "mummies little soldier". Add that to role models who enact power imbalances in the genders, the media, the fairy stories etc and you certainly have a recipe for fully grown soldiers of the future.

Tony Porter a co-founder of "A call to men" which is an organization that works towards ending violence against women by promoting healthier attitudes in all men, speaks very honestly about the "man box" that we put our little boys in. He has lots of videos on youtube and a great website that you can visit to explore these concepts further.

The Man box

1) Do not cry openly or express emotions with the exception of anger.

2) Do not express weakness or fear

3) Demonstrate power and control especially over women

4) Aggression, dominance, protector

5) Do not be like a woman

6) Must be heterosexual

7) Must not be like a gay man

8) Tough, athletic, strength and courage

9) Makes decisions, does not need help

10) Views women as property and objects.

In one of his videos he says "I asked a 9-year-old football player how he would feel if in front of all the players, your coach told you that you were playing like a girl." The boy responded, "It would destroy me! I said to myself, 'God, if it would destroy him to be called a girl, what are we then teaching him about girls?'"

In this same video, he tells the story of when as a 12 year old boy, an older neighbourhood friend, the cool dude who all the young boys looked up to, invited him to have sex with; meaning, rape a mentally disabled 16 year old girl named Sheila. Even though he did get out of the situation without raping her, he found himself pretending that he'd done what was expected of him. Though he knew rape was wrong, he didn't want to be seen as less than a man in front of his friends.

He also said he was conflicted because he knew Sheila was in a dangerous position and needed help, but he also felt excitement because he had gotten away with it!

He says at the end of this talk:

"I need you on board. I need you working with me and me working with you on how we raise our sons and teach them to be men. That it's okay to not be dominating. That it's okay to have feelings and emotions. That it's okay to promote equality. That it's okay to have woman that are just friends and that's it. That it's okay to be whole and that my liberation as a man is tied to your liberation as a woman."

You see, he also said that we teach our sons not to be interested in girls world! If his son had invited a load of girls home to play, his immediate thought would be "which one is he interested in" If it turned out that he wasn't interested in any of them, he would then start wondering if his son was gay. Now, remember the "man box stuff" and all of the judgements on being gay in this world? The less aware among us and our children will actively reject boy's ability to be interested in girl's things. We hear it all the time, "I don't play with girls things" is quite common among little boys especially once they start school.

Harmless enough when they are little, but what does this ultimately play out like?

One half of the human race not listening to or understanding the other half, that's what it plays out like! The other half of course understands the masculine world. We are taught to, it is given value and of course it is attached to our ability to survive and prosper. We also internalize it and often try to become more like it, you know "tom boys" in a bid to become "not like the other girls". This can often lead to a total devouring of the feminine energy such as "women joining the armed forces and even demanding to be allowed to fight on the front line. The ultimate form of internalized sexism!

The subject of domestic abuse is often labelled a "woman's issue". I have heard many people say that men shouldn't be involved. Professional people too! First and foremost, domestic abuse is not a "woman's issue" It is a "mans issue" they are the main perpetrators. It's a bit like saying, racism had nothing to do with white people, they have got to sort it out themselves and we can happily ignore the situation and continue to be racist or be ok with racism. That is ludicrous, it is also victim blaming. Secondly, because of the conditioning, women will listen to men more readily than they will listen to a woman or failing this will often defer to the masculine viewpoint. They also do not often make the mistake of thinking that a person not of the male gender can know it all and they sometimes have the belief that if a woman refuses to buy the masculine cult any more, she must be a man hater and her bias is clouding her wisdom. A prime example among many others I have, is when my daughter exclaimed to me "Mum, Paul told me how men view women as objects and it's made me feel sick" and then proceeded to tell me stuff I had been telling her for ages ☺ When I pointed this out, she said, yea but he's a man telling me! So you see, we do need each other, generally women already listen to men, we need to balance the other side now don't we? Thank goddess for men like Tony Porter who listened and then harnessed the positive masculine energy (which men do so well) and did something about it!

There is a great article on the 1 Billion rising website titled "The man box and the cult of masculinity" by Derrick Jenson. In it he shows that denial of the man box even being in existence is linked to all of us viewing it as "how life is" and so therefore there is nothing different. All other genders and species must conform to the "man box" so therefore it is "the norm". He correctly points out that it is cultural conditioning and not human nature! In effect; "The goldfish bowl water".

So is there a "woman box"? sort of, it fits inside our part of the man box and is called "internalized sexism", or maybe even "the internalized man box" as for every imbalance in power there is the also the other powerless side. Apart from all the other species that are impacted on by this man box, the impact on the other type of human being actually helps hold this dynamic in place. Animals will for the most part not conform to this "man box" and so therefore we are losing so many different species at an alarming rate. Not so cats, dogs, mice, horses, rats, or food producing animals though. These are valued slightly more and/or can adapt to "how it's meant to be" they are useful! The ones that adapt to this environment and are not useful inside this small mind perspective, this masculine value system, will find themselves facing population control. But the woman's role in this largely upholds the masculine values and of course, we are useful, I mean we have babies and look after them don't we? We also have to become more masculine to succeed or gain any independent power and/or we also play the subservient role very well. Deference to the masculine viewpoint and lack of resources will largely create an environment where women internalize sexist beliefs whilst also keeping each other in line and as a consequence hold each other back.

Here it is, "the woman box"...

1) Be loving and cry whenever you can and never be angry.

2) Vulnerability is ok, be very scared!

3) Demonstrate weakness especially around men.

4) Sweetness, subservience, needs saving, must be pretty

5) Do not be like a man

6) Must be heterosexual unless making porn movies for a man but must pretend we don't

7) Must not be like a gay woman unless making porn movies for a man

8) Weak, graceful, fragile, fearful. Oh and; don't fart!

9) Does not make decisions, needs help.

10) Views Men as the saviour and the saviour as a man.

Here's an excerpt from a 1950s home economics text book that was taught in schools, you can kind of see why we support this "Man box" can't you?

The Good Wives Guide

Have dinner ready. Plan ahead, even the night before, to have a delicious meal ready on time for his return. This is a way of letting him know that you have been thinking about him and are concerned about his needs. Most men are hungry when they come home and the prospect of a good meal (especially his favorite dish) is part of the warm welcome needed.
Prepare yourself. Take 15 minutes to rest so you'll be refreshed when he arrives. Touch up your make-up, put a ribbon in your hair and be fresh looking. He has just been with a lot of work-weary

people. Be a little gay and a little more interesting for him. His boring day may need a lift, and one your duties is to provide it. Clear away the clutter. Make your last trip through the main part of the house just before your husband arrives. Gather up schoolbooks, toys, papers etc. and then run a duster over the tables.

Over the cooler months of the year, you should prepare and light a fire for him to unwind by. Your husband will feel he has reached a haven of rest and order and it will give you a lift too. After all, catering for his comfort will provide you with immense personal satisfaction.

Prepare the children. Take a few minutes to wash the children's hands and face (if they are small), comb their hair, and if necessary, change their clothes. They are little treasures and he would like to see them playing their part. Minimise all noise. At the time of his arrival, eliminate all noise of the washer, dryer or vacuum. Try to encourage the children to be quiet. Be happy to see him. Greet him with a warm smile and show sincerity in your desire to please him. Listen to him. You may have a dozen important things to tell him, but the moment of his arrival is not the time. Let him talk first – remember, his topics of conversation are more important than yours.

Make the evening his. Never complain if he comes home late or goes out to dinner, or other places of entertainment without you. Instead, try to understand that his work is strain and pressure, and his very real need is to be at home and relaxed.

Remember it said: "His topics of conversation are more important than yours" and; "don't give a f*ck if you done all this preparation and his lordship f*cks off down the pub with his mates after work"! His work is strain and pressure and he does after all need a place to unwind

and relax away from noisy children, a nagging wife and domestic stress. And he really does not need snotty noses wiped up his best suit when he is just going out with his "bird"!

I told one of my facebook friends that I would be impressed if he said he enjoyed picking up his children from school, meaning for his daily chore. He answered; "That was a rare pleasure, usually at work at that time. When that did occur, yes, I enjoyed it. It was a surprise for the children - one which they very much enjoyed".... I responded with "wonder how much you would have enjoyed it if you were up to your eyeballs in washing and cooking and you had to go along every day and be with a load of women (as a woman not a man) feeling like a bad mum whilst the children and other mums see you as imperfect?"

- I guess a mother who has to do that every day may see it as a chore, yes".

- "What about if she said it was a pain in the arse, and is a thing that gets in the way of her being able to go to work to support herself and her children? Then what about if she is a single mum and all her kids are over 3 years old and she has to answer to the jobcentre why she hasn't got a job and juggle all the chores of running a home and family?"

- "Fuctifino. A difficult place to be. Especially when sanctions are applied at the drop o' a hat"

- "Yup, "Fuctifino!" indeed!"

For those of you who don't know, "Fuctifino" means; "what the f*ck do I know"?

Oh and; here's another rule for the "woman box"

11) Wait until she has gone out of the room before you start talking about her!

I have lost track of the amount of times I have heard and said myself at times too; "what kind of woman is she"? "What man would want her, she's like a bloke"? or "what kind of a mother is she"? or "she's a slag!", maybe even; "God she looks a state, did you see her wrinkles, fat a*se"? Etc, etc, etc!

This impacts on our ability to form trusting loving relationships in groups. Sure we can develop great one on one relationships with other women, and we are really great at caring for each other. But what about if you both fancied the same man? Or wanted the same job? Or she pointed out that your man was not good for you? Or what about if she absolutely extolled the virtues and beauty of another woman to you? Lots of women experience this as the other person saying that they themselves haven't got those virtues or that beauty. And with a lot of unaddressed internalized sexism, you could even begin to find fault in the paragon of virtue and beauty that has just been presented to you.

What about the things we say about a woman who leaves her children!

I have often been asked if it could not be seen as internalized sexism also in men? I don't think it can quite be described as that because these values are given credence by society, I think it is more like straight up "sexism" rather than internalized, sexism. Internalized masculine superiority and privilege maybe, but not sexism. If it were feminine values that led the world and men had to conform to be what suited the feminine energy alone and reject their masculinity as second class, but still act like men in the bedroom and a woman to be able to get on in the world, then yes, but it ain't is it! Hmm... That conjured up quite an image ☺

We also uphold these values in our "preferences" in men. We like a macho man, a hero, you know; the one fresh from the fight! We are attracted to power and status and dare I say it; wealth? This is also, believe it or not; cultural conditioning. I do not exempt myself from this one, in the past. Women can have a tendency to measure their own status based on the calibre of the man they are having sex with. In effect our self worth is often all in our crotch!

I have learned so much about myself and the world that nowadays, I naturally see these types of behaviour or status as "not attractive". I just am no longer drawn to this, plus I know that it is about their weakness and is not strength at all! So give me the "awakened man" any day! The strength and ability that it takes to no longer conform to the "man box", to speak out about it, to nurture their children and to value women does it for me now.

I also do not buy into valuing myself only based on what I look like anymore. Yes, I still have stuff that comes up, like fear of and disgust sometimes at my wrinkles, and I will use makeup if I want to make an impression or I am feeling down about my looks. But for the most part I am now quite content to grow older more gracefully ☺ I was never satisfied with my looks anyway, even when I was in my prime. When I look back on old photos of me I can clearly see just how beautiful I was, these are the same photos that used to make me cringe with horror! So no point whatsoever in that was there? Nowadays, makeup free, I can clearly see my own beauty, not sure anybody else can, but that doesn't always matter anymore. I can remember a time in my life when pretty much everything had collapsed and I had lost so much but I looked in the mirror after doing my makeup and just thought; "well it don't really matter, I still scrub up well, I still got a chance of finding a man"!

So you see, we can change can't we?

5 COVERED IN SKIN

So, is this just a male female divide? Absolutely not!

This same or similar dynamics play out in isms of any kind on different levels of severity. Race, class, size, wealth, culture, behaviors, religion etc. Even species(ism) at its most subtle. The list is endless but is always subdivided at the same time by the male/female position.

Think about what that might do to individuals in any of the groups. On the one hand they are seen as superior because they are male and on the other hand inferior because of their class, culture, race, size, wealth, age, behaviors etc. This creates huge splits in the human psyche as people grapple with their subconscious worthiness and unworthiness issues.

This produces what is known in the psychological world as "splitting". A simple definition of this in the dictionary is: The separation of one item into two so that they can be handled separately, like; chopping a log into two so that it can be picked up to throw on the woodpile. Unless you pieced it all together, you would not see the tree. So connecting this to the "as without so within" concept, it means separating two contradictory thoughts or values that are otherwise uncomfortable, if you like; thinking in boxes. Thinking only in boxes does not enable resolution of complex ideas and often over simplifies. A most common split that occurs is separating things into good or bad. The good part can then be valued, whilst the other side is either repressed or attacked.

There is nothing wrong with splitting per se as it is essential to the learning process. To understand something in more detail, you need to split it. A good example of this is the domestic abuse dynamic in the last chapter, you know, male, female differences and the fact that domestic abuse is a product of fear and/or hatred of the feminine energy. Whilst the male female split was essential to start with, it must then also be combined with lots of other ideas once the truth is uncovered to build a more complex picture of the human race, i.e. how all the logs fit together to reveal the tree. The problems happen when we try to put things only in boxes and label them good or bad. When you understand the complexities and the simplicities of a subject you are able to assess each situation more accurately. So that the fact that it's not always men that are doing the hitting and it's not always the woman that is being hit, does not then become the detail that scuppers the truth.

Splitting is also part of growing up in a "f**ked up world" where we are told things are good or bad and where we eventually become adults and can look back and see that things were not "all bad" or "all good" and learn to handle life. If this stage doesn't complete children may grow up with a polarized view of the world. All good in this for instance could play out in its most physical manifestation as the "Pollyanna" effect I think, you know; "love and lighters" and all bad being the "privileged one" who blames everything and everyone for their adult experiences. Think about how splitting also might manifest as bipolar in extreme case of flipping between high and low. Perhaps even think about the person with depression who can see no good in anything in their life. This is of course <u>all</u> very f**ked up thinking and labeling anything as "good or bad" from the bigger spiritual perspective can be seen as a challenge you need to overcome. But to enable exploration of this we need to consider how it plays out in this version of the human race.

On this dysfunctional planet, psychologists tell us that splitting is a symptom of defense against feelings of love or hate for the same object. So you might have split your mother into two i.e. good mum/bad mum. She is good when she is being or doing something you like and she is bad when she does other things that you don't like. The therapists job is to help the person realize that they are doing this and to help the client see that "mother is both good and bad, she is still the same person and that is the reality of the world" ??? I have quite a few issues with just leaving it there. It's a great start but accepting that mother is great sometimes and a total a**hole the next and just saying "that's who she is" doesn't go far enough to heal the planet of mistrust or even our value system of good and bad. It is great for accepting so called "good and bad" in self and others, as long as you understand that the good or bad is only the result of your value system which has been created by a masculine cult that actually makes us all wrong! It also contributes to the divide and rule dynamic that is keeping the system in place. Yes we must learn to accept our own and each other's so called "foibles" but we have also got a chance to recognize that we are all "f**ked up" and need to start using those said "foibles" in a positive way towards positive ends instead of having a go at each other with them or because of them.

A prime example of this split in thinking in a relationship that creates cognitive dissonance can be; the victim of abuse who sees the abuser as a "good father". I used to say this myself and others (minus the details of abuse when telling others of course). My children's father often mentally, physically and emotionally abused me in front of them, even included them in the abuse, yet I still thought that because it was me that was "taking it" he was leaving them alone and they would be alright.

We all have lots of internal voices that will have been rooted somewhere in our past, they reappear in full view when we are scared or depressed or excited or happy or going without some basic human need or comfort. We also put them inside the minds of the "empty vessels" we consider our children to be. Sometimes they conflict each other, just like one of mine where I saw and heard my children fearful and crying whilst I was having the sh*t kicked out of me and they heard me being yelled at, whilst being the recipient of the violent dysfunctional behavior; "Look what you are doing to your children" he ranted as I curled up in a ball...

Once the storm had passed and dad was now telling mum to make a cup of tea, they resumed their play as if nothing had happened or went back to sleep. I used to look at them and think "Phew! At least they are alright now, nothing bad has happened to them". I knew nothing of the impacts of the childhood on adulthood. I used to tell them "hitting a woman is always wrong" yet I stayed, I couldn't get away so I had to disassociate from the full horror of the situation. Talk about cognitive dissonance, the belief that whilst he abused and controlled me in front of the children he was still a good father often comes back to haunt me with guilt, I had blamed my own Father enough for my own predicament! Although I was just blaming him at that time for being such a tyrant that I had run away from my childhood home a few times before finally leaving as soon as I was able and had ended up with a violent man. I knew nothing of subconscious conditioning in those days. I even used to say "Well I got hit as a child and it never did me any harm"!

Yes my children's father did some good things for them, but we all lived in fear and uncertainty. I was conditioned in some ways to believe that children needed a father no matter what. I was certainly fully conditioned to believe I needed a Man, not only conditioned but was immersed in a culture that played it out too!

These "thought splits" in their most extreme form play

out as schizophrenia It is a relatively common defense mechanism for people with so called "borderline personality disorder" and "psycopathy" and in their positive use as an ability to deal with the world and help us understand the details of all parts. It is also in its darkest form great for thriving in a position that requires zero empathy or sympathy like "banksters" and "Gangsters"!

I am not surprised when I hear that people who have been diagnosed with schizophrenia are also often very sensitive souls. I think if I was less of a "Masculine warrior" within my psyche, I would have gone stark raving bonkers by now. I would probably need to totally disassociate too! And even create a "fantasy world" if that is indeed what people with schizophrenia are doing. I can see the reality of defending against love here.

I remember when I had my first baby. I was overwhelmed with feelings of love like I had never felt before and at the same time a massive great big fear of losing her. So much so that I cried for days after she was born. I prodded her every 5 minutes or so just to make sure she was still alive. As time went by and more children come along, I was not quite so bad with the fear thing, the love was still strong but the fear had subsided a bit. Then imagine I had known about how addiction to power and control and this splitting tendency could actually be capable of manifesting much worse evil than I can take on as "likely". Also put that to fear of authorities taking your kids, your lowly status, and seeing it in all its glory. Then perhaps think about what it might be like to live as a human in a human family and care about every member of that race as if they were your own child. Then just to make it even more difficult, what about if we loved all of the other species on our planet in the same way? How would you be able to cope?

I f**king wouldn't, that's for sure!

Then think about how "relative safety" can make you feel less afraid, as long as your loved ones are ok then you are able to cope and to just love them; f**k everybody else!

"Yea, we need to launch a strategic attack on Libya", I heard one deluded caller say to George Galloway MP. "A strategic attack!" Said George, "Do you know what a strategic attack means? It means dropping bombs down on people's heads, that's what it means caller!"

We love our own children and would defend them with our life, yet we are not screaming and shouting in defense of or falling on the floor with grief over those Libyan kids or the Iraqi kids are we? A defense against love? I should say so! How would I cope with the powerlessness if I loved those children in the same way as I love my own? How would you? How much do we dare to love? How much do we have to disassociate from the full horror to be able to cope? How trapped do we feel in a system we believe we can do nothing about?

You see, the domestic abuse dynamic, and male/female split is just a situation that is playing out, to show us how the world is operating in its condensed form.

As a mother, I had been fiercely protective over my children and even as they became adults and had children of their own, If they were in problems I wanted to fix it for them. You see, if they were not ok, then I was not ok! My parents had never been like this towards me and so the pendulum swung too far the other way. Then it changed, I realized that this wasn't helping them, one particularly dark time when I threw my arms into the air with despair and demanded an explanation of why they couldn't cope like I always had to! I immediately realized I had only been flexing my own "coping" muscles, I wasn't empowering them to believe they could do anything or even find out how to do it for themselves. So I stopped doing it so much, they thought I had stopped caring. God if only they knew the amount of guilt frustration and fear that brought up in me! I love them dearly and I was willing to sacrifice my own need to be ok and let them struggle. I started trying to teach them my spiritual knowledge and use the training I was receiving to try to help them. It didn't work! They just saw that as more rejection, it all became very f**ked up as their fears around me not loving them became their reality. It is moving forward now and I have every hope for the future. But at the time I felt absolutely powerless and helpless; but I know they will one day see...

Once I realized this disempowerment dynamic, I was kind of stumped!

That's when I decided! If I could do nothing within the role of "mother" to help my children to see the way, then I would have to change the world! I didn't know how I was going to do it, I did not have a clue. I just knew I would go crazy if I wasn't trying to do something. So I threw my heart and soul into my teaching on a pretty single minded mission to find out how to change the world for my children and my grand children.

As I hadn't come up with this concept totally at that point, I was still pretty split, you know, believed it was a crap environment and we had all been affected by generational abuse and things that happened in our past. I knew internalized sexism and racism were at the root of it, but never really thought that people were so disconnected from this that we wouldn't all change it as soon as I made them aware of it. Even though I understood the fact that we pass our family/cultural hurts/beliefs on generationally, I really thought that it was only the ones on the bottom it had happened to and the ones further up and at the top would be horrified once they knew what I know (even those right at the top) and would want to change the world.

I still believed in the "Great white hope"!

I had been at what is often considered "the bottom of society" I had lived with the so called "Druggies, unemployed and criminal classes". I had lived for most of my life before this in the "gypsy culture". Oh man! Backstabbing, competition, mistrust, grassing each other up, scared of being grassed up, strong fighting man culture, beating, controlling and owning women among all the other things "dysfunctional" environment caused, were plain to see. I am not saying "Gypsies are more dysfunctional than anybody else" I am not even saying the lifestyle is more "dysfunctional" than any other (I think living in square houses and working for the man until you die is so much more dysfunctional than that) I am just saying, it was plain to see, it was clearly in the goldfish bowl water and seen as normal, not really hidden. A ray of hope here though! Because it was so "in ya face" the younger generations are seeing it more and more easily and are now changing that. The changes always start to happen, when it is no longer a "closed shop".

I am not saying there was nothing great about my travelling lifestyle either. Imagine living (relatively) free from bills and accumulated debt. Imagine living in a community that largely knew that the "sh*t life was in conforming to the system" Imagine waking up in the morning in an orchard with cherry trees in full bloom, sitting on a cherry stump under a tree whose branches sweep silently to the ground to form a kind of majestic living flowery gazebo. Whilst watching the dawn slowly kiss and silhouette the blossom and the leaves that surround you. Earthy, dewy grass smells lingering in your senses as you listened to the early morning feathered arrivals, who you knew you were going to be in battle with later, but for now they were just a few song birds. Sipping a cup of tea, fire crackling in the background, sweet smelling cherry wood smoke adding to the aroma as it curled through the blossom and leaves and you smoked your first fag of the day, heaven...

Anyway, I digress! I am just saying "The crappy stuff was on full view". Even talked about openly and prescribed. I have heard it said on many occasions when a woman was being 'unruly'... "Beat her"... coming from out of the mouths of the other women.

Not a lot of trust flying about either.

What about the so called; "Druggies and piss heads?" We were something else! Dependent on your level of addiction and access to resources, robbing from your own grandmother and children to supply the next fix is pretty common. Violence and crime and death and destruction are the order of the day in its extremities. The harder the drug, the bigger the buzz, the lesser the morals! Not because addicted people start off any worse than the rest of humanity, it's just the attraction to the flame you see. A bid to reconnect to that "something else" that is so elusive and can't be defined, yet the power of the buzz feels a bit familiar, so you keep searching. You know there is something missing from the "normal world" but you just don't know what it is. You just keep searching for it until you discover that whatever it is, it is not at the bottom of that bottle or in the contents of that syringe.

And then you find it! It's called transcendence...

When I surfaced from my sleepy perception some 17 years ago and saw my 20 year relationship for what it was, I got the f**k out of there as fast as me little legs would carry me! I was heading for the respectable world. I was going to mix with people who didn't shout and cuss each other down, didn't beat women, trusted and supported each other. I was going to find peace and self esteem. I hated having to do things that were considered wrong in society; it scared the crap out of me!

The same theme 4 years later, when I woke up from the substance addictions and arose from my detox, I couldn't wait to meet all the beautiful people and live in the "Promised Land"!

Not so my release from "working for the man", this time I knew there was no wonderful world already prepared and waiting for us. This time I really knew, we have to create it ourselves, together!

My experience in my last year at university shocked the hell out of me. I had been metaphorically dragged into the head of schools office by my ear! I was questioned rigorously about my past criminal record information, told I must behave myself, told I must report immediately to them if my "behavior deteriorated" What??? They could shove that request right where the sun don't shine! They would have been the last people I would have told if that had happened! It also (in their minds) shifted the achievements from me to them. You know, I only changed myself because they ruled I must, nothing to do with the beauty of my own soul and morals!

I was also told very "benevolently" that they were not going to ask me to leave the course.

I felt totally humiliated! And pissed off at the same time. Where had all the lovely people gone, like my other tutors in the previous years? Like the people who worked at Mind? Like the people who worked at surestart? These people had been "in awe" of my journey and my valiant struggle and supported me to achieve healing.

This new lot? F**k me, they were like a bunch of strict superior tutors at a school for delinquent teenagers!

I think they later tried to "cool it" and treat me as an adult, but it didn't really come across too well. Hence my antics on this final year that I wrote about in my first book.

I was telling a very dear friend about this and I was most indignant! He remarked; "you sound shocked". "Yes!" I said, "bloody right I am shocked! These people are "up there", they are counselors, and they work in the caring professions! They should know that rules are counterproductive! They are pretty much at the top of the teaching ladder! They do not have to struggle like me"!

"That ain't what you normally say", he responded. "What do you mean, not what I normally say"? I probed, "well, you normally say, the ones on top are the worst" …. Stunned silence as I struggled with this truth. Then I got it, my developing realization about the system being the problem and it getting worse at the top was actually turning out to be bloody well true!

Later a dawning realization as I connected it to something a student remarked when I was teaching them how to develop the "ethical moral qualities" required for a counselor to practice. He said "Wow! A recipe for world peace!". That was it! My mission was set!

 I still had not connected the full understanding. I still thought it was just worse in the ones on top. Even though I knew that there is such a thing as a continuum, even though I didn't realize this was what I was doing, I still thought in good and bad, bottom and top.

I still believed in human's ability to really care about others and also their ability to unite and work together to change this by changing themselves. I was going to work hard to bring this knowledge into my workplace and together we would change the world. It was of course, a total f**king projection!

The more I woke up and realized that this was not going to happen, the more frustrated I became even at one point getting really frustrated and heartbroken as I watched my dream die and the people around me not seeming to care enough to actively do anything much about anything. I saw the fear as in desperation I gradually became a rabble rouser and they thought about losing their jobs! I saw some of them in total denial that anything was wrong with it. I also saw some people's irritation as I threatened their cozy existence. One person even tried to teach me that I needed to do what they do; "At times of great abundance, do as little as possible, then when the squeeze happens as it inevitably must in a capitalist system, you do not get over run with work as you get it piled on your lap because of financial cuts". I was appalled! What?? This is a recipe for keeping the world as it is or shutting it down and does nothing for the students experiences or the organization! I was also equally appalled to see the fear that was instilled by management, who I am not really sure understood that was what they were actually doing and the fear and slaving ability that emerged from the teachers and admin staff as this time, now the squeeze was looking like becoming fatal.

I could clearly see that communication and cultural issues were adding to our workload enormously, I could also see the impact of this on our ability to recruit students. I offered to train the whole workforce for free! My own courses, after 5 years of development were successful, the students (from all different cultures) really developed as a community that respected and assisted each other to get on in ways different to how things had started. By the end of each year there was a higher level of developing camaraderie and a real understanding of personal responsibility in relationship to others, a respect for the journey of others and the world. I offered to teach the workforce how to expand for free too by including past students and giving them the work experience they are lacking, I had a plan! Management listened and did nothing! They even eventually started to block what we were doing within the counseling and social care section; they used the excuse of financial concerns and insurance.

It started to dawn on me as I was brought to realization that these people thought in boxes (totally in their left brain) and had no understanding of broader and deeper concepts whilst having a discussion about whether or not the moon can affect our emotions, and speaking to a work colleague. She was the head of the organization I worked for actually, who stated categorically that she did not believe that we are affected by the moon. I asked what she thought about the fact that we are made up of 80%ish water and that the tides are affected by the moon. She said; "it doesn't affect us because we are covered in skin" (Gob smacked!) This led on to being very symbolic i.e. the way we judge ourselves and divide along gender/race lines, related to what type of skin we are in. The way others judge us. The fact that lots of us think we are separate from nature, you know that superior streak we tend to have over other earth beings, preferring to think that we are the only ones with consciousness. The issues of racism and sexism colour of skin and gender, still very much present on the planet, not to mention the ever present class divide. I realized she wouldn't understand any of it, even though one of her most reiterated statements whilst talking to the whole service on inset days was "We must remember that everything is interlinked, we all affect each other"! The final straw came whilst having a conversation with another work colleague about our relationships now being all about need and dependency. The next boss down from the top who happened to be in the staff room butted in: "That's a huge generalization" she said! The contempt on her face when she said this flipped a switch in me. Rather than go into an explanation about generalizations (like I usually do) I retorted; "And sometimes privileged people are unaware of the impact of themselves on others around them!"... The way she responded left me in no doubt that I was now f**ked! She looked at me with confusion, turned on her heels and left...

By this time I had become totally consumed by my mission. The planet was falling apart and this lot gave no more feeling to that than if we were talking about my washing machine breaking down! I hadn't put the "world peace thing" to them but I couldn't get them to care about their students and staff at that point, so the rest of humanity was out of the question. I was so bloody frustrated I had just been trying to help but they didn't understand what I had been trying to tell them. This was a public form of "telling them" too sometimes, like on stage at whole service personnel gatherings. Me and my dearest friend Nikki usually received resounding applause from the workforce; some of the braver, brighter ones even, before I left, started to do the same thing. In the beginning, management would applaud too, before they had time to think about what I was saying that is (It took them 5 years☺)!

I thought they would understand! I thought they were benevolent souls, I thought they would get it and I thought I could help...

 Once I realized that they were in the way of saving the service, and the planet of course ☺ I could often be heard ranting and raving in the office. I remember somebody saying to me once "It might be a good idea to learn to take it in your stride!" I ranted back: "I am used to taking things in my stride, I am a woman"! (He was a bloke) It is very, very easy to take it in your stride when you don't give a f**king sh*t, isn't it!

I knew there was another way! My multi-cultural students were making my courses and their contents well known and being great role models in their communities and across the globe. We could expand and we could do so by utilizing the "free resources" that were being offered by past students as Work or practice placements. Both myself and my co-tutor (dearest friend) Nikki could then be free to do what we do best and more of it too. There was another way. We didn't need this pyramid, we could spread out in circles. It was a vision!

But, like I said; they would not listen, and the rest of the workforce were for the most part; "just doing a job".

By this time I was beginning to work unethically, I was getting close to fitness to practice issues, and burn out. As management would not listen to any of our concerns and they constantly wound my students up by continually chucking them out of their class room, because they wanted it for a management function/party/training course etc…

They did lots of other things too like; not providing them with anywhere to eat their food other than a room not much bigger than a small dining room in a small house, it was right next to the toilets (The toilets were actually bigger than the room) Imagine that one! Some days as many as 30+ students trying to find space and keep out of the way of the procession to the toilet and receptionists telling them off if they ate in the classroom. It was a special building you see, it belonged to crown estates (the queen) and it was just off of Regent Street. Our senior management team were addicted to it! I couldn't help noticing that when management were using the classroom for their "gatherings" they always had food in there. Even offered my students their left over's for having commandeered their classroom and benevolently allowing them to eat these scraps in the classroom as a treat to make up for the inconvenience (So bloody short-sighted).

It didn't seem to matter that most of these students had paid over £3000.00 to be on these courses!

The less other people seemed to care, the more I ranted in a desperate bid to get them to see what was happening and at least give my ideas a chance and my students some respect. My supervisor, my co-tutor and my line manager eventually helped me to see that I was so affected by stress that I was not making safe decisions, I was working unethically. I went out sick! As much as I am addicted to being involved in changing the world for the better, I am not so stupid as to believe that it can't happen without me. And rather than do damage, I would relinquish the thing I loved. A bit like the real mother in the story of king Solomon ☺

In my burnt-out, frustrated, guilty and stressed state, I thought I was pulling a fast one. Having time off work because I couldn't cope with the task, in my past experiences, meant you didn't get paid. I was getting full pay! I felt guilty as hell at leaving the students behind, but the only way we could have got the course to completion and enhance my colleague's ability to continue to work there was to shift the responsibility of one of the hugely work overloaded level 3 Access groups onto somebody else whilst she coped with the two full time counseling groups, one of which was just a level 2 with a smaller amount of work attached. I had already written all of the plans for the rest of the year and so this lightened her load a bit. It didn't actually happen like that because they lumped the whole lot onto her for a while because nobody else wanted to or could do it and the awarding body kept demanding more perfection! The following year she ended up "wounded in action" as she did the same as me and pushed herself too far. All in our bid to survive, look after the students and the organization, whilst being criticized for not being good enough, and trying to help heal the planet!

Sound familiar?

This is when it truly hit me, these other so called "civilized class cultures" were worse than the cultures I had run away from! They might not be openly brawling and cussing and stealing and holding each other back, but it was the same dynamic, just they did it in other ways and pretended they didn't. Way's that couldn't at first be seen had fooled me. Fools them to this day I think!
I have learned my lesson with this one now though. My exit ended up in the same way as my first exit from the abusive relationship. I left my children in the first one and my students in this latest one.

I was totally done! For about 5 months I had no energy whatsoever. I am on the tail end of that dragon now and just starting to recreate a vision.

Another really relevant sign here to finish the chapter; I clicked on facebook after I finished writing that bit and this was the first post I saw:

"How can one of us be happy if all the others are sad?"

An anthropologist had been studying the habits and customs of this tribe, and when he finished his work, had to wait for transportation that would take him to the airport to return home. He'd always been surrounded by the children of the tribe, so to help pass the time before he left, he proposed a game for the children to play.

He'd bought lots of candy and sweets in the city, so he put everything in a basket with a beautiful ribbon attached. He placed it under a solitary tree, and then he called the kids together. He drew a line on the ground and explained that they should wait behind the line for his signal. And that when he said "Go!" they should rush over to the basket, and the first to arrive there would win all the candies. When he said "Go!" they all unexpectedly held each other's hands and ran off towards the tree as a group. Once there, they simply shared the candy with each other and happily ate it. The anthropologist was very surprised. He asked them why they had all gone together, especially if the first one to arrive at the tree could have won everything in the basket - all the sweets.

A young girl simply replied: "How can one of us be happy if all the others are sad?" The anthropologist was dumbfounded! For months and months he'd been studying the tribe, yet it was only now that he really understood their true essence... [ix]

"Africans have a thing called ubuntu. It is about the essence of being human, it is part of the gift that Africa will give the world. It embraces hospitality, caring about others, being willing to go the extra mile for the sake of another. We believe that a person is a person through other persons, that my humanity is caught up, bound up, inextricably, with yours. When I dehumanize you, I inexorably dehumanize myself. The solitary human being is a contradiction in terms. Therefore you seek to work for the common good because your humanity comes into its own in community, in belonging." -- **Archbishop Desmond Tutu**

Food for thought!

6 WHEN TWO WORLDS COLLIDE

One really prominent "macro" example of the race/culture "split" began its descent into hell some 522 years ago in the "Americas".

During my investigations I had come across the work of ˣDavid E Stannard and brought his book; "The American Holocaust"... It really opened my eyes and I saw just how vast the extent of my own conditioning was...

The opening chapters in this book tell a very different story to the one I had always believed or rather, never questioned. It was only when I shone a light on these so called "facts" that I realized I had thought that way. I had largely been conditioned to believe that the spread of colonization had occurred on mainly unpopulated and empty lands where just a few scattered uncivilized, free roaming and savage tribes lived, scratching an existence in the wilderness and never developing any structures. In effect you could say that without realizing it I had formed an opinion that they were not much more intelligent than the animals! They had no towns, no cities, no education, no civilization, no history. They were also "all the same" or rather "one type of culture" although I knew nothing of the concept of culture in those days. These new found people were just backward, needed civilizing and we had done them a favor, we brought technology and resources and an advanced peaceful way of life. In essence, we had saved them! (A reflection of Freud here) I believed this of

Africa, of India, and of Australia too. I didn't know about all the other places then, but my simple belief picked up from the little bit I learned at school was that; Civilization had spread from Greece and Rome and the Romans had brought it over to England and civilized my ancestors and then we spread it around the globe.

This book spoke of a multitude of diverse cultures across the Americas that whilst vastly different, lived quite happily side by side. There were all kinds of terrain and weather conditions and each culture developed around the environment that they lived in. Some lived in towns and/or great cities, some were farmers living in communities, some fishing communities by the water and some lived in hunter/gatherer cultures even populating the frozen lands of Alaska etc, etc, etc. They had superior systems of clean water, sewage and canals, they were really, by all accounts a much, much more diverse and advanced civilization than the Europeans, who's so called "civilized" ancestry dates much later than the much older ancient civilizations they had found that they ironically called the "new world"! Who were in fact much more advanced thousands of years earlier than the Spaniards were when they found them. And I might add, who actually <u>were</u> "all the same"! Or rather came from the same poverty stricken patriarchal divided culture as the rest of Europe.

No civilization? Not one that the Europeans cared to write about anyway!

As we know, the victor always writes the history, it is no surprise to me that the official "history" of colonization largely sounds the same, it goes something like this:

"A few small groups of savages have been found roaming around in unclaimed virgin territory with no civilization to call their own. We sent out missionaries to help civilize them and the ungrateful bastards turned on us because they could not be domesticated. Ultimately we became their victims and so they had to be eradicated".

This happened all over the world and it became such a theme that I couldn't help but notice the similarities.

When the Spaniards first made their way to the Americas, they found a land of peace, beauty, abundance and hospitality. They were amazed at the technology, the magnificent structures, the cleanliness of the people and the surroundings and the people from all different types of cultures who were healthy, loving and giving. There were also millions and millions of them!

David Stannard wrote:

"Just 21 years after Columbus's first landing in the Caribbean, the vastly populous Island that the explorer had renamed Hispaniola was effectively desolate; nearly 8,000,000 people, who Columbus chose to call Indians had been killed by violence disease and despair"!

How did a few boat loads of Spaniards manage to kill off

all of those blood thirsty savages? The answer is really quite simple; they were not savages. They were peaceful and welcoming, knew nothing of warfare and trusted the Europeans. An excerpt from a letter Columbus wrote clarifies this point:

"They are artless and generous with what they have, to such a degree as no one would believe but him who had seen it. Of anything they have, if it be asked for, they never say no, but do rather invite the person to accept it, and show as much lovingness as though they would give their hearts."

He also wrote:

"With 50 men we could subdue them all"

This would surely not be a description of a people that were vicious and warlike. In direct contrast to this we can compare the society of the Europeans:

"The Spain that Christopher Columbus and his crews left behind was one of violence, squalor, treachery, and intolerance, in this respect Spain was no different than the rest of Europe" Stannard (1992)

He also goes on to explain in detail the historic events that led to the bloodthirsty, sadistic and savage destruction of the native people. He states in his convincing and extremely well researched book that this destruction and dehumanizing phenomenon has and is still being carried out among the Native American and indeed the black descendants of slavery and in diverse indigenous cultures across the world. At the time of writing his book he noted;

"In South Dakota, where Indians constitute about 6% of the population-as elsewhere in north America- the efforts to destroy what remains of indigenous cultural life involves a greater degree of what Alexis de Tocqueville described as "America's chaste affection for legal formalities". Here the modern requerimiento[xi], pressures Indians either to leave the reservation and enter an American society where they will be a bereft and cultureless people in a land where poor people of color suffer systematic oppression or remain on the reservation and attempt to preserve their culture amidst government imposed poverty, hunger, ill health, despondency and endless attempts of federal and state governments land and resource usurpation" Stannard (1992)

In other words, they must fit into the "man box" or else and even if they did most of them would be f**ked! When considering the different cultures within the parameters of Narcissism, sexism, racism, superiority and splitting. With its connection to domestic abuse, it could be argued successfully that not only did the Europeans bring with them, pestilence and genocide, but also their culture of domestic abuse and denigration of the woman. This is very much still going on today, in A United Nations press release in 2002, on Human rights, slavery, terrorism and women, the following was stated:

"One non-governmental organization, Minnesota Advocates for Human Rights, said the roots of violence against women were complex and related to women's traditionally subordinate role. No country was immune from the plague, which resulted in such offences as discrimination and harassment, domestic violence, sexual trafficking, and rape. Strong patriarchal cultures and

negative stereotypes combined with the priority given to economic issues continued to block improvements in security and equality for women". United Nations (2002)

This is also backed up by a recent report from Amnesty international where Native American women were reported to experience more abuse per se, and they were let down by the government on every level the report stated that;

"It is time to halt these human rights abuses that have raged unfettered since this country was founded." (Amnesty international 2007)

With this and all the rest of the background information in mind it does not seem surprising that;

"In terms of causation, European American women tended to say that domestic violence was caused by personal, internal dysfunctions of the abuser, such as anger control issues and abuse had always been in their culture, whereas American Indian women viewed the cause of domestic violence to emanate from society and social problems, such as poverty, unemployment, and lack of mobility due to isolation and it was not in their history". Tehee and Esqueda (2007)

This next excerpt from this investigation of cultural differences that interviewed women on domestic abuse stated:

"In addition to the open-ended responses and the attitude measures, American Indian women offered comments concerning

domestic violence that were not part of the actual interview process. These responses indicated the occurrence of extreme violence in their lives and the responses to violence they would take. For example, several American Indian women mentioned murder and death as outcomes of domestic violence, and some mentioned women they knew who were in jail for defending themselves against domestic abuse. They reported the use of retaliation as a possible response to domestic abuse.
European American women never mentioned such information, even with additional inquiries about such events". Tehee and Esqueda (2007)

To Sum this up, the horrendous case of Kevin Annett who uncovered genocide of the Canadian natives (Film: Unrepentant) when speaking of the societal impacts on Native people who were living with extreme abuse and violence within their culture, he was asked "What do you have to say about this?" he replied; *"That's what Genocide looks like up close"*.

You see, it gets passed on!

Kevin Annett uncovered that when Native American children were forced from their families put into *'boarding schools'* and taught the culture of the Europeans, they were beaten, sexually abused and murdered... It wasn't actually just there that it happened either. These children's death camps are to be found all over the world! We are just starting to uncover them in Britain too
Do you think this might be perhaps where the Native American abuse dynamic began? You see, abusive systems eventually require less violence to continue,

thus becoming self perpetuating as the survivors forget their history and start to conform and get "quietly" abused. Perhaps this could be evidence to support the Native American view that their culture does not have historical abuse against women. It started with the invasion of the Eurocentric cultures. The European American women thought their culture had always been like that! In effect, they had no belief that once long ago, their ancestors might have been reverent of women. If you believe there had never been "another way", then you might not fight it too much either! Just like the fish in the bowl doesn't want to change its water.

Unless it gets too murky and it starts to be uninhabitable. Then it might start gasping for air and know there is something wrong with it.

Lots of things were at play in this culture clash where projections and parallel processes acted out in a horrific eruption of power and control madness. But there were "trigger points" where misinterpretations added to a speeding up of the genocide and enabled the "victors" to excuse and justify their own behaviors.

Have you ever wondered where the term "Indian giver" comes from? The natives bestowed many gifts onto the new arrivals freely and lovingly. The Europeans, after first of all reveling in the hospitality must surely begin to become suspicious of this. They knew nothing of projections did they? The mistrust would have started to

grow and parallel processes would certainly have begun to play out. Just because Freud or Bernays weren't around in those days, doesn't mean the subconscious wasn't, not recognizing your own assumptions is easy, especially if it is trauma based!
Stuff would have come up like; "What are these people up to? What would they be expecting in return? You don't give gifts for nothing, even; "these people are too stupid to understand how to capitalize on their abundant resources"... The natives gift giving culture may well have been enhanced by a belief that the initial invasion of the Columbus mission was a prophecy happening and they were celebrating. But it was still an expression of the culture, we wouldn't do that if Jesus arrived on the scene would we? It is not in our culture. I think we might even name him as a terrorist and shoot him, he would even probably be banned from the church!

The Europeans did after all come from an exchange culture and a monotheistic system. Then of course, the Indians who largely lived within an intricate system of "gift giving" expected the Europeans to share out the gifts equally among themselves. When they saw them hording they realized that these leaders were "sick" (mentally ill) and not able to redistribute and share so they took it back and redistributed it. Both sides would have started to mistrust each other! Of course it escalated rapidly for the Europeans because they were used to mistrust, it was in their culture. Remember that other ability we have to project past experiences into the future that keeps us out of assessing accurately just what is going on? A culture that had largely no need to mistrust because of the gift giving principles, would take much longer to wake up to danger don't you think? Remember that one that we do when we think "<u>They</u> wouldn't do that" and we put ourselves in danger because "<u>we</u> wouldn't do that"...

What about the fact that most if not all of these cultures had a reverence of women, so the community structure would not have been in place in the same way as patriarchal structures? What about the fact that they largely lived with their ancestors? The burial mounds were mainly prominent in their environment. Think about how people who live with a sure and certain knowledge of spiritual infinity would view death differently than those of us who are not really totally sure our loved ones have survived on the "other side". We might have a belief because we had been told but no real experience like the native population have. A great example of this cultural "knowledge" still in existence today is on an Island called Balut-Saranggani a small agricultural and fishing community south of Mindanao, Philippines, where people celebrate with great joy, the death of a loved one. There is music and laughter and many joyful words spoke about the person who had just died. They experience as a reality you see, that their loved ones have made the great transition. Death is not an end to life, there is no such thing! They have simply moved on, to a position where they can watch over the living and play a role in supporting their destiny. They celebrate the joy of living and it is seen as the ultimate respect you can pay to the departed. How might somebody from a culture where death is associated with endings, loss, sadness, uncertainty and grief view these "foreign people"? Disrespectful maybe? Or uncaring towards their dead perhaps? Savages maybe? Think about it, they didn't even speak the same language! What about the lack of "shame" over their sex lives? How might that be viewed as evil by "puritan" thinking people? How might the fact that some of the native groups had never organized into farming communities or built structures and developed technology, merely living off the land, be seen as backward by the Europeans? You know "no civilization" just roaming aimlessly around. They failed to take into account that actually, these were the absolutely successful ones, they had achieved full balance with nature and had no need to work! What about the fact that they could not get them to work for money or riches? Could they perhaps have seen them as lazy?

How about the belief we have in the sanctity of the "masculine right of spiritual ritual" where only the men can perform certain rituals, where women are seen as "not pure enough" or important enough. In many cases to do with the judgments our religions pass on to women connected to the time of the month. Even if it is not a "religious" doctrine or punishment in your belief system, it is certainly a subject that we largely see as "dirty", maybe even shameful and we hide it, even calling it "the curse"! Then what about if you stumbled upon cultures where only men use the "sweat lodge" (a spiritual ceremony) and women as a general rule did not? Might you think that in this culture, the men were the important ones, just like yours? What about if they could not explain to you that because a woman purifies naturally once a month, she does not need to do the ceremony, she is a pure, spiritual being because she purifies naturally from the inside out? This ceremony is about purifying from the inside out and men need some help with this, women don't. Then even if you could get that concept, how would they get you to understand without you maybe wincing, feeling a tinge of shame or thinking "yuk" that they adore and revere the monthly bleeding! Especially if they couldn't talk your language! Think about it, what sort of body language actions might you need to do to get your explanation across on this one?

Then think also about difficulties in cross cultural communication even if you do speak the language. We have a tendency in "individualistic" cultures to value lots of words in our explanations. We absolutely need to in fact because we have pretty much lost our connection to each other. Knowledge is seen as "owned" in western culture, we have to pay for it! We also do not often talk about our deepest knowledge with each other because of fear or mistrust of others outside of our group. We even judge a students' knowledge and give them grades based on how much detail they can give about a topic. Basically this translates as "the less somebody has to say about something, the thicker they are". Think also about how the more we get to know each other, like close friends, the less words we need to help us get a concept across. We develop a kind of telepathy with the other person as one word can actually mean so much. We do not have to add the details; we have usually shared all of these details often with our close friend as we experienced it. Our knowledge grows together. Now this is a very important difference for people that come from cultures that are collectivist. They share knowledge, it is important for the groups comfort, evolution and survival. Because of this they develop words that have deeper wider meanings and so therefore manage to say much more with fewer words. Well, those Europeans could certainly be accused of thinking the natives were "stupid" or "thick" and this different speech context would certainly have highlighted a point and helped them make assumptions. The person from a culture that assumes that others do not know the knowledge that they are about to impart uses lots of words (Individualist Low power context) and could view the person who is assuming group knowledge and using few words (collectivist high power context) as not knowing much. In other words Thick! This certainly still happens today, so think about how these early Europeans might have jumped to conclusions... Savages they called them didn't they?

They would certainly have lots of reasons in the relatively few examples I have given here to justify their treatment of the natives that was driven by poverty induced greed and a sense of superiority. Remember that the addiction to power and control and the "man box" was nearly as strong then as it is today. You can read more on cross-cultural differences in a book called "Conflict across cultures" By Michelle Lebaron and Venashri Pillay and watching videos on youtube by Native American activist Russell Means.

Are you seeing all of the parallels here to the abusive relationship? What about the way our systems are driven today? David Stannard wrote about the "blotting out of knowledge" of the indigenous people and cited Frantz Fanon:

"The colonialist reaches the point of no longer being able to imagine a time occurring without him. His takeover of the colonized people, is deified and transformed into an absolute necessity"

For the glory of god and the chosen people!

Of course this is for the civilization of the savages too who god sent these invaders to save! Then they act out the "victim" role of settlers seeking freedom from their own oppressive governments and wear the cloak of courageous pioneers of a brave new world. They of course, totally buy this version of their history because there is a lot of truth in it from their perspective. They did flee a culture of violent control, and because they knew no other way, they just created it somewhere else. Of course they had fled tyranny, if they hadn't learned it and saw their subconscious conditioning as "normal" then the destructive systems wouldn't be in place today would they? We would all be at peace, wouldn't we? The destruction of the native population is a blot on this "wonderful flight to freedom" of the past and might spoil the whole perception and so the horror needs to be denied or repressed. Splitting and cognitive dissonance occurs, parallel processes play out, the past is projected onto the future and Cultural myths develop that sanitize the truth and protect them from the shame or guilt they might feel if they faced the full horror. As time passes, these myths become part of those beliefs that we never bother to examine, why would we? No sense in digging up the past eh?

A total reflection of how masculine heroic superiority plays out! It's in our governments, it's in our education systems, it's in our places of employment, it's in our relationships, in our fish bowl. It is one gigantic big parallel process and it all fits nicely into the "man box". There is a great [xii]video on youtube called "How America Is like A Bad Boyfriend" that cleverly shows the parallels between our relationship with the patriarchal system and the abusive relationship. It could just as easily be called "How the Europeans were like a bad boyfriend"

Before any of us start pointing the finger at the descendants of those that did this, it might be worth considering that actually, it happened all over the world even to the Europeans. Britain was invaded by the Romans remember? We are actually all descendants of survivors of genocide and have had our cultural history rewritten, we just passed the abuse on and forgot about it.

I can see plenty of reasons to dig up the past; it will show us a way that has been buried, a way where we can all get along but first of all we got to get past our own guilt, it helps to uncover the brainwashing...

In the opening paragraphs of David E Stannard's book he draws a parallel between two acts of patriarchal destruction in all its glory:

"In the darkness of an early July morning in 1945, on a desolate spot in the New Mexico desert named after John Donne Sonnet celebrating the holy trinity, the first atomic bomb was exploded. J Robert Oppenheimer later remembered that the immense flash of light, followed by the thunderous roar, caused a few observers to laugh and others to cry. But most, he said, were silent. Oppenheimer himself recalled at that instant, a line from the Bhagavad-Gita:

"I am become death, the shatterer of worlds"

There was no reason to think that anyone on board the "Nina, the Pinta", or the "Santa Maria" on an equally dark early morning, four and a half centuries earlier thought of those ominous lines from the ancient Sanskrit poem when the crews of the Spanish ships spied a flicker of light on the wind-ward side of the island they would name after the holy savior. But the intuition, had it occurred, would have been as appropriate then as it was when that first nuclear blast rocked the New Mexico desert sands. In both instances (at the Trinity test site in 1945 and at San Salvador in 1492) those moments of achievement crowned years of intense personal struggle and adventure for their protagonists and were culminating points of ingenious technological achievement for their countries. But both instances also are a prelude to orgies of human destructiveness that, each in its own way, attained a scale of devastation not previously witnessed in the entire history of the world. Just 21 days after the first atomic test in the desert, the Japanese industrial city of Hiroshima was leveled by nuclear blast; never before had so many people (At least 130,000, probably many more) died from a single explosion. Just 21 years after Columbus landed in Hispaniola 8,000,000 had been killed. But what happened on Hispaniola was the equivalent of fifty Hiroshima's and Hispaniola was only the beginning! Within no more than a handful of generations following their first encounter with Europeans the vast majority of the western Hemisphere's people had been exterminated".

How murky does our goldfish bowl water have to become before we gasp for air, look back to a cleaner environment and find another way?

7 SEEKING TRANSCENDENCE

Alcohol abuse and alcoholism have caused compounded problems for American Indian and Alaska Native peoples. In addition to all the other stereotyping as "primitives" we now see "Drunkards" added to the list. Most modern day studies of drinking among American Indians have focused on the people living on reservations or on traditional Indian lands, even though many maintain sober and relatively productive lives in mainstream society.

Before European colonization, there is no record of addiction to alcohol even though they did produce it; they generally used it for ceremonial purposes.

As the death and destruction of the native people developed, so too did their addictions. There are all sorts of theories relating to why this happened i.e. The Europeans were not good "drinking" role models, the alcohol was stronger, the Indians didn't have time to develop healthy and moral guidelines related to alcohol after it was introduced, even something wrong with their genes! Among other things that create a smokescreen, these theories are put forward as a cause and are largely forgetting the impact of genocide. Indians already had alcohol, how come there was no known history of addiction pre-Columbus? Substance abuse was common among the invaders though and I wonder too if it might not be the effects of their own genocidal experiences both as victims in their long forgotten past when they were ripped away from the bosom of the "mother cultures" and as perpetrators of horror in those extremely violent times. We have been told that no regulations around its use and strong encouragement by the Europeans created a "tradition" of heavy drinking among the natives that is still in existence today. Maybe we might discover something about the impacts of abuse, if we stopped making up daft excuses to salve our conscience.

I find it an interesting connection that the natives called it "fire-water" and in my own journey I have discovered that my addictions were linked to "attraction to the flame" and not being able to find what was missing.

What about the other issue of "mental health"! Statistics will tell us that there is a higher incidence of schizophrenia among "non white" people living in European countries that are not their "homeland". There is also a figure of 67% of Native Americans, especially women (living in urban mainstream culture in America) who are diagnosed with mental health issues. This is also true of the Irish population or any other population of non-English people who reside in England. The incidents of "psychosis" among black people from the Caribbean is higher still!

For a start; mental health sickness, including but not limited to, psychosis, schizophrenia, bipolar and depression are all, over diagnosed in Western society. We must remember that the "roots" of psychiatry developed at the same time as slavery and colonization was at its highest. Mental health sickness is seen as a "problem with the organism" i.e. something is wrong with the person (the environment is largely fine). The way these are categorized and defined are not the same as physical health sickness. If we are physically unwell it can be detected pathologically i.e. blood tests. Mental health cannot be diagnosed in this way. Those of us who believe that they are caused by chemical imbalances in the brain, might want to go ask your doctor if it you can have a chemical detection test on your brain. He/She will tell you there is no such test! The categories and symptoms of mental health are decided by a panel. Yes that's right, psychiatrists, mainly from white upper middle class backgrounds will decide what behaviour is abnormal and give it a name. That's it! No tests, not much individual exploration of circumstantial abuse history or culture, just a vote on the masses! A psychiatrist called John Breeding, the student of Thomas Szaz the Hungarian born American psychiatrist who was the preeminent voice of psychiatrists around the world, a number one critic of his own profession, has quite a few videos on youtube for those who want to explore this concept further.

I have included a task I did at university in the appendix[xiii] that shows how this western belief system that we live within can easily create misdiagnosis. We were asked to choose a fictional patient and show how mental health assessment works both from the perspective of the "assessor" and the "patient" ☺ I couldn't resist!

When I have given this to students in the past, a large percentage of the "non-white" students "get it" straight away and can even relate incidents of this happening with their own families and friends. The main objection I get of it "being "over the top", or "not likely to happen" come from "white middle class cultures"... Very telling in itself that one!

There is no such thing as the (mental health) medical model in Native or "Eastern" cultures, it is largely seen as a sign that somebody is "emerging" and they are taken through a spiritual process whereby they emerge later as a "guru" or "wise one".

I find an interesting connection to myself here, when I lived at the "bottom of the pack" where there is unrecognized abuse by the ones further up I got addicted to substances. Once I moved into the so called "wonderful world" of mainstream society it became all about "mental health"!

For the past 55 years I have lived life managing to keep away from being diagnosed with worse than normal mental health sickness. I got diagnosed with depression a few times once I had escaped the "in ya face" abuse but there was this one time I had been very lucky! There was one major episode in my life when I could have come unstuck big time, if I had not been fortunate enough to be refused treatment from my doctor because in his eyes all of my behavior problems were related to substance abuse and, they don't do anything much with duel diagnosis anyway. When I had my cathartic experience, my daughter thought that I was just 'on something'...

As far back as I can remember I have always been a quite expansive "thrill seeker", even as a child. One of my mother's phrases still resounding in my ears, sometimes to this very day is; "Mandy! You always go too far you do"! This was true, and always has been I suppose. I can remember many episodes in my life when I have pushed conventional norm's and just did whatever seemed like a good idea at the time, either to escape from the awful circumstances at home or to discover something. Like; eating some wild berries just to find out if they were poisonous or not. The aftermath of that one was not pleasant as I found myself later being forced to drink salt water and suffering the indignity of having my dad's fingers 'nicotine flavor' shoved down my throat! Whilst this was quite a mild episode in comparison to the many other adventures I had as a child, I think it illustrates nicely what was going on for me. If it was considered not done' by others, or things were unexplained and whether or not I was conscious of this, I often done it. It never occurred to me to give the consequences a thought. All that registered with me was, "I wonder what this does" or "that looks like fun". I always wanted adventures and I never had much fear. On another occasion I can remember swimming in the sea with my rubber ring firmly in place, about 5 years old and feeling like I could swim forever... I think I was wondering how far I could get and where it would take me if I kept going, "MANDY" resounded in my ears and startled, I lost my concentration and began to slip from the ring. Within a few minutes I was being dragged back to shore in a most undignified way, like a wet rat in a rubber trap, by a bystander who had heard my mother's panic and leapt into action. Boy was I cross! "You showed me up, you nearly drowned me"! Was all I could say to my mother as I marched up the beach feeling excruciatingly embarrassed as my dream of finding faraway lands and making a bid for freedom slipped away... I felt stupid and not one bit like a hero, it took me all day to forgive my mum for that!

As I approached my teens it got worse and my attempts to create fun with my friends and escape from tyranny at home, found us more often than not in trouble big time! I was usually the one that copped the blame, and it was not unheard of for my friend's parents to stop their kids hanging around with me because I was a bad influence. A bit unfair really because the way I remember it was that I wasn't always the one that came up with the hare brained schemes, although I was often the one in front leading the way, so they can be forgiven for thinking that I suppose.

The point I am making in all of this is that I was an original 'free range child' needing adventures and fun and excitement and never quite making it because I usually got caught or stopped or taken advantage of in my openness to adventure. On many occasions I can remember lying in bed as a child feeling really bad... usually after being told off or recovering from a thrashing from my father. I never did set out to knowingly break the rules, all I can remember happening is that I could feel the energy rising as I was getting up to something or other and just going with it. It was sometimes like being on an exciting fairground ride that I couldn't get off of and wouldn't have wanted to anyway. It took me away from what was happening at home. I felt different to everybody else; I was always looking for a laugh or even a buzz' just to remind me I was alive in the awful abyss of normal. In my younger years this materialized itself as breaking rules and doing things unconventionally, like catching a horse and riding bareback through the fields, feeling the wind blowing through my soul and being free, enhanced by the fact that I was living in the moment and the ridicule and control my father had over me was not in my awareness. I didn't see it as wrong, I thought the rules were stupid anyway, they were the bad guys not me.

The result of this was that I was often in trouble and sometimes spending time on my own after one of my adventures had been discovered and contemplating my badness. It wasn't that I saw my actions as wrong, quite the opposite, I just soaked up all the awful ridicule that was aimed at me by my father as he told me how stupid or dirty or disgusting I was even when I hadn't done anything wrong. I believed him, he was my dad and had no reason to lie, I thought…

I wanted to be a good girl, I didn't want to be a bad girl, and I always helped everyone I could. I just wanted to be involved with people in a closer way, but I just became a pest, or not really accepted. Trouble is with this one, the part of my nature that is accepting, giving and forgiving started to get the better of me and I took on a sense of responsibility for everybody else's feelings. I couldn't stop doing so called 'bad' things because I needed to feel alive, I was interested in so much, and I wanted to experience everything, so I just concluded that there was something wrong with me! And as most everybody else said... I was out of control. Searching for transcendence...

I couldn't handle the sad feelings either, I cried and cried at the thought of my family eventually having to die. Alone in my bed at night I would sob my heart out, I wasn't afraid of dying myself, I just didn't want to go through the pain of losing the ones I loved. This led me on a quest to try to discover whether there was life after death... strange really, for a child so young. I would ask everybody I thought might know, like teachers or vicars or even the police! And when they explained, I can remember saying "Yea but how do you know that's true"? One explanation that did go some way to teaching me about the afterlife was told to me by a young vicar. He said: Imagine a load of grubs at the bottom of the pond, all wriggling about in the dark grimy mud. Then imagine that the time comes and one of them floats off to the top of the pond and is never seen again. The rest of the grubs all start crying and missing their friend. They don't know that he has turned into a beautiful dragonfly and is flying about in the beautiful bright sunshine that they cannot see because of the mud and they will see him soon enough when they become dragonflies themselves. This stuck with me and I even use the analogy of the insect metamorphosis to describe the process of change within my counseling model to this day. I still cried at the thought of my loved ones all dying before me and leaving me in the mud though. My mum even took me to the doctors over it. He totally misinterpreted my fears and told me I had a long way to go before I died, he hadn't taken on board that I was scared of feeling the pain of loss of those I loved, not worried about my own expiry date! The point that I am making here is that I really could not handle the sad feelings, the huge amount of love I felt, and boredom made me want to explode! So as a child I was constantly filled with emotions that led to devastation or 'mad-ass' behavior, more 'mad-ass than devastation I might add in my younger years...

Sensitive, they call it! Or Emotional! Adding further to the feelings and thoughts that something was wrong with me, I didn't handle emotions like others could. My friends could certainly hold their tongues better than I could. And then there were the 'rages', god, when I got pissed off, I really got pissed off and whilst for the most part, I was a peaceful soul, I could fly into monumental explosions when everything got too much. So at age 17 I felt like I wasn't good enough and would be 'left on the shelf' and jumped at the first offer... although this was also made more attractive by the fact that he was also promising an unconventional life, running away with the ones' who still lived in the old way, a trailer, alongside the road, on a farm, in a field, fires, living outside, now that was something I could really get my teeth into!

This descended into a life of extreme abuse, where I further developed my energy sensing radar in order to survive and still be a bit crazy. It's a good job that he spent most of his time in the pub or I could well be "shut down" or even dead now. His absences allowed me to express this further and also the life of ducking and diving and breaking the rules that goes with the "on the road gypsy culture" as a survival mechanism, added further fuel and kept me sane. Or rather, insane from the perspective of this society. I was often up or down with my emotions and the bit that kept me level was the control that he had over me through fear either for my own life or the life of others that I loved. Plus the huge amount of work I had to do, no time to feel your emotions too much when you are run off your feet eh?

However, once I escaped from that relationship and the culture, there was no fear again; in fact my experiences had made me more fearless. My need for transcendence took over once more and I found the dubious 'delights' of alcohol and drugs... this was like the best buzz on the planet (at the time, it don't last long before you need to up the danger) and I can remember wondering, at the height of my substance abuse, why everybody else wasn't on drugs, even remarking at one point that they should treat depression with morphine and I believed it.

By now the emotions had really taken hold, I was on anti-depressants, that seemed to make it worse but I still thought they were helping. I thought I would be worse than this "worse" if I stopped taking them (stunned silence here) and I was either very up, or very down... sometimes these episodes lasted for days and whilst to the outside world I appeared to be level sometimes, I could kick off with an 'up' outburst or a 'down' outburst, depending on what the underlying theme was.

My kind of 'mania' saw me doing many, many nutty things as I sought out the thrill of high emotions. I could get giddy just thinking about doing something different. My addictions were all part of this and I never consciously became an addict to drown out my experiences, far from it, I never really was one to bear grudges or cry over spilt milk. I became addicted seemingly for the hell of it and took higher doses trying to reach the heights. Nowadays I realize, I was searching for transcendence from oppression. I became dependant on it, sure I did, but the reason for getting addicted was because I was looking for transcendence not really because I couldn't cope. I wanted to live! Hell I was out of control and my drug/alcohol fuelled escapades were bloody crazy... When I became a street drinker, even the street drinkers couldn't put up with me and I felt different in that too as even they shunned me because I spelt trouble.

As the time went on, my addictions continued until I came to the point in my life where I was shunned by my whole family, the one daughter that still lived with me hated me and I had no friends left. I wanted to die and when my doctor told me that I wouldn't last the year out, my thoughts were "good, thank god for that, it can't come soon enough" as I put the glass of brandy to my lips...

A couple of years into my training, I was talking to my tutor about my inability to handle my own emotions in my younger years and she pointed out that it showed that I feel things in more depth that others... What did she say? I feel things in more depth than others? Not 'I can't handle my emotions like others', bloody hell, here I was all my life feeling really inadequate because I couldn't deal with my emotions and all the time what it really meant was that I had a harder task because my feelings were huge and I hadn't shut them down so much as lots of others had. Well, well, well! That makes a whole lot of difference I hadn't thought about feelings being on a continuum, to me sad was sad and happy was happy... well bless my soul, it all made sense, of course... it goes with all the other extremes too, now I was really making sense of what was happening and had started to see myself differently, in a more favorable light.

Further on in my training I began to study mental health and actually began to work with people with severe mental health sickness in a drop in. As I was reading about the different aspects of the sickness and working within the dynamic, it slowly started to dawn on me that the symptoms of bipolar and psychosis were actually very like my own experiences... You know, the stuff we do when researching medical symptoms, we have all the fatal ones at times don't we? Oh dear! Did this mean that there really was something wrong with me? bloody hell, I had better get this checked out so I duly went along to my doctor and quite matter of factly announced that I think I have got Bipolar, to which he set about arranging for me to be seen by the psychological services!

My understanding developed and I was introduced to the continuum... bloody hell, I worked out the symptoms of all mental health distress could be viewed from either end of the spectrum, so for instance bipolar at one end of the line is feelings on a massive scale, and no feelings on the other end describes people with little empathy and who can be considered as in lots of cases to be high achievers, narcissistic or even psychopathic with no drugs available. Meanwhile on the other end (Bipolar) is a severely debilitating phenomenon that is treated with powerful drugs that in some cases render the patient incapable of normal life! It gradually gets closer to each aspect along the line from the middle which is considered normal functioning. I soon discovered through my investigations that this was the same with everything as well as all the disorders. At the same time discovering in my counseling practice that all of my clients with severe mental health sickness had roots going back to abuse and their experiences of mental health sickness usually paralleling their experiences of abuse along the two continuums... very interesting. This is the reason when later we were required to create a fictional case study on a client with mental health sickness from the perspective of the mental health professional and also the perspective of the client I got an even bigger awakening.

I chose a black 35 year old male and duly wrote about his symptoms using the DSM 1V (diagnostic manual) I quickly had him sectioned and on heavy sedation because of his symptoms and actions. The other side of that from his cultural perspective told a very different tale! The symptoms were also indicative of spiritual emergence (Kundalini rising) and what's more they also matched my own episode during my "self imposed" detox, well as you can imagine I was gob smacked... what the hell? Further research left me convinced that the western view of mental health sickness might be wrong; after all I had survived a so called "psychotic episode" without treatment and come out the other side a 'wise woman'!

Like I said in the eastern view as there is no such thing as mental health sickness, rather the person is seen as 'special' and taken through a process of spiritual treatments where they emerge the other side as 'cured' but not just cured as a Guru or spiritually developed person and revered!

This left me all over the place and I wrote in one of my assignments:

"This module has left me questioning the beliefs and sciences of the western psychological perspective in connection with mental health dis-order and when working with client's who show signs of psychosis, I would feel happier referring them to a witch doctor instead of a psychiatrist, something that I don't think we have referral sources for at Mind; but I would have to, because it is the rules in my profession, refer to psychological services, something that I would do with much fear now because I know that the chances are, they get worse from here on"

After finding this out and realizing the treacherous slippery slope that starts from the psychiatrists consulting room, I never followed through on my enquiries about my own mental health sickness; that was a close one. I remarked about it after discovering this, that if I had been treated by the doctor during my detox, my symptoms would have most likely been linked to psychosis and I too could have been sedated and for want of a better word, STUFFED! I would not have been working at the mental health drop in; I would have been a service user…

But getting back to the feelings; in personal development as a counselor the aim is to "really" get to know yourself because of transference and energy interactions, and it also covers the strange phenomena of acting like the other person is expecting you to and is related to figures in the clients own life that I wrote about in earlier chapters. So for instance a client may be viewing me as in some ways like their mum, and I find myself acting in or feeling certain feelings towards them connected to the 'mother' role. This is a good tool in counseling as it allows you to feel possibly what is going on for the client; it's a great exploration point. But I have also observed another type of phenomena in my colleagues as sometimes they appear to become' each other, and often seen it in myself too although this one is harder to define. One particular incident was talking to a friend after she had spent a lot of time with another colleague and she made a comment about peoples actions, she was quite harsh as she said it (more befitting of a comment made by the other colleague) whilst the other person came out with a comment that was kind and accepting, more likely to have been made by my friend and really not like her. I spoke to my friend later... "What the hell's up with you" I said, and remarked that she sounded like the other person. She replied, "Do you know what, I didn't even think that, I don't know what made me say that and she said what I would be likely to say normally, I just felt really spiteful at the time I made the remark... now I feel really bad!

Whoa! They had swapped places during that brief moment and began to act this out. I have since observed this everywhere and also began to tune my radar into what's going on in the underlying interactions with me and others in everyday life. Of course we always have to remember that we all have every ability in us, so it's ours too, perhaps not so readily useable but it's there... So their wound meets our wound and we swap our energy.

This realization all came together for me and now I know why I have felt so odd all of my life. I have usually been able to see deeply into what was going on inside me in my interactions with others and felt most of the crap that was being directed at me, and for the most part before my training, blamed myself for causing a bad feeling. So I concluded that I did all the crap, not just some of it, it was all me! I pick up quick on what is going on and what could possibly happen. This sometimes leads people to back away from me in lots of cases and in others to attack me as they got unintentionally (or sometimes it was intentional) 'dug out' by me. The less kindly people that do not know me well have often shunned me, they get over it if they stick around and sometimes even if just for negative intent, not really being comfortable with my presence. The ones that I could really connect to were the more intense souls and the sweet souls, or the needy ones. My favorite ones to be around were the intense ones; they tend to exhibit more passion and of course as a result of this and living in a reserved society where the 'stiff upper lip' is the norm, if not nurtured well in this, tend to act crazy, just like me.

So my madness is directly related to my passion, my ability to love and intensity as the reserved-ness' of this society oppresses me and, not to be caged, I have in the past had to thrust myself into the heights of craziness in attempted transcendence and I have been carrying other peoples stuff for years and blaming myself for being a horrible person; perhaps the openness to others had sometimes allowed an energy swap that I acted out

(Like, I am sure other people felt bad, when they kindly acted out my crap and I got away with it ☺). So of course I have felt different all my life. I am bloody different, we all are, none of us can really define ourselves, because we might be acting on somebody else's wound eh?

So to sum this up... I relate more to the experiences of people considered as having mental health sickness and much less to the stiff upper lip brigade and my counselor training has taught me how to embrace my feelings and thoughts more each day. These are more closely linked to the shamanic views both in mental health and society and my experiences now allow me to accept my feelings more, express my wilder side in fun when it feels right, sometimes have a big fat rant when it feels right too and throw my passion into trying to make some headway with this in my quest to help heal the world!

We got a great big long way to go until we recognize (mainstream) that the real "sickness" on this planet is linked to "no feelings", no empathy, taking and not sharing (hoarding resources) and competitiveness, oh and a crazy obsession with industrial time. I laughed when I heard a colleague remark that the lunatics have taken over the asylum in reference to the mental health hierarchy and some silly rule... and very seriously quipped back "The lunatics have always been in charge of this asylum" and I am now sure of that!

So I'm not mad really, or suffering from mental health sickness, just got more than the "acceptable" or rather;

"normal" share of connection to feelings, i.e. not so shut down. Sometimes it's bloody difficult being able to love life and others in this "f**ked up world"... You know; "If you don't give a sh*t you can contain it"!

So you see, it is easy for me to understand that rather than being "something wrong with the person" it is the environment that causes all the "ills" because I have lived as a loving being whose biggest desire was to connect to others and belong! I have experienced the disconnect of not living with a loving "tribe" whilst still being able to keep my feelings open... It eventually sends you crazy and sometimes makes you drink!

Imagine what it must be like for people who can still remember that connection to others and the hopelessness they might feel at being overrun by a group of people with the mental health sickness of "hoarding possessions" who see them as second class humans! Imagine the horror of being a survivor of genocide and still trying to keep the culture of a broader and deeper love connection to others alive whilst being misunderstood, lied about and blamed! Imagine!

Then think about the way we try to resolve issues in a patriarchal system; we make rules! You cannot rule against pain!

In 1832 American congress passed a law banning the sale of alcohol to Indians. It was repealed in 1953 and tribes were given the option of retaining or rejecting prohibition on the reservations. Today at least two thirds of the reservations are "dry" yet there is little difference between them and the ones that still continue to allow alcohol. In fact the problems increase because the "drinkers" on the reservations were more susceptible to death or injury when drinking in mainstream society outside of the reservations.

If rules solved problems then my job as a counselor/teacher would be easy! I could just sit clients down and tell them what to do!

That is laughable!

8 FUCTIFINO

So in the early years, I had started off on my foray into the "wonderful world" that I believed was in existence, only to find out it was a totally upside down belief. I believed it so strongly in fact that every time I was presented with evidence to the contrary, I searched my soul and wanted it not to be true! I even largely acted on my belief that my new found knowledge was wrong about the general population and quite often came unstuck in my trust that humans were "not uncaring, judgmental or unkind". I still have a part of me that really wants to be plucked out of this experience and woken up to a "real world" where women and men are equal. Where masculine energy is not more highly valued than feminine, when all of the things that I have discovered suddenly turn out to be a delusion on my part and the world really is a wonderful place not riddled with isms where you are not seen as equal unless you are the right color, size, age and gender and came out of the correct vagina. You know, a bit like the matrix in reverse; I want to be wrong! ☺ I am always open for this to happen! It's part of having an idealistic soul! It also helps me to explore these concepts more thoroughly and make up my own mind as I experience this for myself without the impact of my own expectations getting in the way.

It makes me wonder why I can see it so readily and

others sometimes can't, then I remember the "past life" stuff I was exploring for a while. I totally understood the idea that the likelihood of having past lives was probably more factual than the concept of biological nothingness. But I also hung doggedly on to that doubt, so much so that I cannot just let myself believe! I have had past life regressions and always come out of there thinking I had made it all up! I wanted to believe it but my cultural norm is of "no physical proof = no sale" The things I put into my past life stories were actually very prevalent in my life today. This creates a real dilemma for me in my bid to think one way or the other. But one thing that really sticks in my mind is the fact that I would be very well suited to living in a gift giving culture, my life (this time) played out in similar (much, much lesser) ways to the history and coping mechanisms of a destroyed people and I added it to my friends comment when he had said "you were a native American in a past life". He also said, after I sent him an old photo of me dressed up as a western saloon girl:

> "My Shawnee Indian friend would say you were 'born away from the tribe' for some reason that will become apparent"

I often wonder if this is the "reason" … If you come from another culture you can see the differences in this one more clearly and are less likely to make mistakes if you are not already sure that something is so. You see, most of my conditioned beliefs were gradually dismantled and my conditioned view of the world changed. I still feel quite lost in this past life one sometimes. The evidence all seems to fit but there is no definitive proof yet for me. I know there are people on this very planet who have had near death experiences where a life review happened, who also talk about the likelihood of past lives, they are totally convinced and very convincing, [xiv]Dr Eben Alexander being a prime example of this. He had a near death experience of his own and as a neurosurgeon had often told patients who experienced these phenomena that it was a hallucination from the brain. He changed his mind after going into a coma where his brain was biologically incapable of creating any hallucination and having one himself! You might want to check him out he has loads of videos on youtube and a great website that explores consciousness from a scientific perspective. [xv]Dr Jim Tucker and Dr. Ian Stevenson have done much research on the concept of past lives and have uncovered many cases that are pretty compelling. I still get stuck on my belief about me though! It's kind of like that thing I used to say when I was young, you know; "My Grandparents were Indians" To feel important or different, similar to; "my dad's a policeman". If I totally swallow it, I feel like I am just trying to be "important" like "who the hell do I think I am"! So it continues to simmer. I am very aware that we can pick things out to make them fit; our researchers do it all the time! Because I know this, I allow the evidence to speak to me whilst I build up a picture. One of the connections I have added to this is my absolute love as a child of "Aesop's fables" a lovely book that speaks of moral messages using animals. I loved it and I kind of put this to the Indigenous philosophy of being part of nature and understanding the signs. I remember clearly the story of the tortoise and the hare and my own experiences of being big headed and rushing things that always go wrong. Whilst if I am slow and steady and don't focus on competition, I usually come up with something great.

I am so glad of that early book and find it interesting that I chose it above the usual fairy tale princess stuff. I did however love "Beauty and the beast"! I loved the thought of her great beauty and love managing to heal the beast of all of his scary behaviors and turn back into a prince because of her love for him and his love for her. I also find it interesting that its one of the top favorite stories of women who have been or are in abuse.

A very powerful clip from a documentary called "The [xvi]Mickey mouse Monopoly" illustrates how popular cultural messages in magazines, on the TV, in our fairy stories play a big part in an adult's life and stem from early socialization. In lots of ways Beauty and the beast will carry a very romantic version of how relationships play out. For instance it shows that a woman must be supportive and patient with her man whilst he tames the beast in himself. These messages are very dangerous when there is abuse in the relationship. He also held her hostage in isolation from her family because he needed her so much. Her own father sold her down the river to save himself! He shouted and scared her one minute and the next he wined and dined her. This is not of course the only way you could view this, for instance. Some "adults" may see it as in this comment taken off of

a domestic abuse teaching website

"What are the types of partner abuse we see in this clip? "

There is no partner abuse in Beauty and the Beast because Belle is the Beast's prisoner, not his partner. Things only change between them when Belle escapes from the castle and the Beast chases after her to protect her, and risks his life to save her. After that, he is no longer abusive and makes a concerted effort to control his temper. That is a defining moment of the movie - when he starts to do things unselfishly for her and commits to changing himself. And no, the message there isn't 'if you love a man you can change him from an abuser to a good person'. There are two reasons the Beast starts to change and neither of them are 'Belle's constant unwavering caring attitude and faith in him despite his abuse': First, because Belle is the only person in his life whose opinion has ever mattered to him (since she is the only one who can break the spell), he is forced to reflect on the way he behaves and try to modify it. Second, Belle is literally running away to escape him and get away from him forever (ie, NOT hanging round changing him) when he decides he is willing to fight wild wolves and possibly die to save her. His motives are clearly mixed, but that's the moment you know that he's starting to care for her and that something is changing about him - right as Belle is LEAVING. In other words, it's HIS developing love for HER that changes him. Also, when he starts to love her he stops being possessive and controlling as a direct consequence of his love, telling her that she may leave the castle. There is no indication in the film that if a man loves a woman he will try to control or possess her; in fact, the opposite message is clearly conveyed by juxtaposing the reformed Beast with Gaston, the villain who wants to force Belle to be his trophy wife. This isn't Twilight: the whole point of the movie is that the Beast is doomed to be alone, to be physically a beast forever, unless he stops being an abuser. I don't know how that can be seen to 'normalize partner abuse'.

A good point! And in an ideal world that would be wonderful, wouldn't it? Women would be the ones who help the men to change by not playing the game of power and control (the man box) anymore. It does however miss the fact that for a start, the film is a total enactment of the game and domestic abuse is a trap, in other words a prison and thirdly "abusers do not change because of their love for one woman. They have also been known to become the persuader i.e. I have gone downhill since you left and your absence is killing me. Couple that with all of the other messages and normality's in our system and it is part of the melting pot that we call sexism, think about the good wives guide here and all the damsels in distress that need a man to save them in our fairy stories and films. Consider also that the above comment from the website is quite a sophisticated concept for a child to understand, they usually just internalize simple messages that they can relate to their environment and it becomes part of their subconscious. Especially if the role models (parents) are in extreme abuse or even just patriarchal led families. This is the same subconscious that drives our automatic thoughts and subsequent actions. They are very likely to internalize the abuse message rather than the other one! And even if they were able to work out in "adult think", the complexities that are covered in that website comment, they are still being set up to accept this as "normal" in men.

You see, in reality the "unhealthy" male does not change for the love of one woman. Abuse is a cycle where there are times of forgiveness that lead on to another episode. In effect, once he has her back, the abuse starts again.

The changes only occur when the abuser develops a love for "womankind" not just one that he wants to posses.

You see, abuse has been normalized in our cultural myths and blame of women and responsibility for the comfort and emotional welfare of men has left us all pretty susceptible to the abuse dynamic and a persistent denigration of the woman's role in this world.

Think about how we are conditioned in this and how it can affect our mental health. Three of our so called "mental health sickness" diagnoses that I do feel are very relevant and play out in our mainstream culture and I truly believe are caused by patriarchy are as follows:

1) Narcissistic personality disorder.

> *"Not unlike the sociopath, narcissists without proportionate successes will demand (either overtly or covertly) to be recognized as superior. With striking similarity to the narcissist, the sociopath is nearly always male and they "place self-interest above all other considerations and are masters at rationalizing their actions, the responsibility for which they often attribute to someone else" (Nance, 2003, pp. 85–86).*

A persuasive pattern of grandiosity (in fantasy or behavior), the need for admiration, lack of empathy. Beginning by early adulthood and present in a variety of contexts, as indicated by 5 or more of the following:

1) Has a grandiose sense of self-importance (e.g. exaggerates achievements and talents, expects to be recognised as superior without commensurate (adequate) achievements.

2) Is preoccupied with fantasies of unlimited success, power brilliance, beauty or ideal love.

3) Believes that he or she is special and unique and can only be understood by or should associate with, other special or high status people (or institutions)

4) Requires excessive admiration.

5) Has a sense of entitlement (i.e. unreasonable expectations of especially favorable treatment or automatic compliance with his or her expectations)

6) Is interpersonally exploitative (i.e. takes advantage of others to achieve his or her own ends)

7) Lacks empathy: Is unwilling to recognize or identify with the feelings and needs of others.

8) Is often envious of others or believes others are envious of him or her.

9) Shows arrogant, haughty behaviors or attitudes.

As with every other so called "mental health sickness", the continuum will be at play and some level of each of these are in existence in all of our psyches and are not exempt from use for "healthy" purposes. It is after all a product of the environment and not a problem with the organism. You will often find that these qualities are more readily acceptable in men and indeed are more prevalent in their most acute form in males and people at the top of the tree! If a woman displays them (at any level) she is much more likely to be attacked for it. Mainly by other women who are often riddled with internalized sexism or rather; seeped in "the man box"!

One of the major obstacles to change for overly narcissistic individuals is their perception that their problems are caused by others rather than by their own self-centred tendencies. This is often accompanied by a desire for revenge and not much realization of the "Impact of the system" or "the man box". In lots of cases preferring to blame the victims for not upholding the system that they believe is right. I have included an article in the appendix that is quite clear as an example[xvii] that is quite fitting.

The second one is most appropriate, even though unsurprisingly enough it is not included in DSM-5. That might just be something to do with the compilers of this manual believing that this behavior is "normal" or perhaps they do not know it exists or it might even be too simple for their over-intellectualized brains? Or what about maybe, they believe that domestic abuse is about masochism? Domestic abuse is mentioned under lots of different headings and diagnoses but it really is quite a complicated process to link all the ideas together to form something that is concrete and simplicity is something that "intellectuals" often run away from like:

"Stockholm syndrome"

(Taken from an article entitled "love and Stockholm syndrome, the mystery of loving an abuser)

"On August 23rd, 1973 two machine-gun carrying criminals entered a bank in Stockholm, Sweden. Blasting their guns, one prison escapee named Jan-Erik Olsson announced to the terrified bank employees "The party has just begun!" The two bank robbers held four hostages, three women and one man, for the next 131 hours. The hostages were strapped with dynamite and held in a bank vault until finally rescued on August 28th.

After their rescue, the hostages exhibited a shocking attitude considering they were threatened, abused, and feared for their lives for over five days. In their media interviews, it was clear that they supported their captors and actually feared law enforcement personnel who came to their rescue. The hostages had begun to feel the captors were actually protecting them from the police. One woman later became engaged to one of the criminals and another developed a legal defense fund to aid in their criminal defense fees. Clearly, the hostages had "bonded" emotionally with their captors.

While the psychological condition in hostage situations became known as "Stockholm Syndrome" due to the publicity – the emotional "bonding" with captors was a familiar story in psychology. It had been recognized many years before and was found in studies of other hostage, prisoner, or abusive situations such as:

- Abused Children
- Battered/Abused Women
- Prisoners of War

- Cult Members
- Incest Victims
- Criminal Hostage Situations
- Concentration Camp Prisoners
- Controlling/Intimidating Relationships

In the final analysis, emotionally bonding with an abuser is actually a strategy for survival for victims of abuse and intimidation. The "Stockholm Syndrome" reaction in hostage and/or abuse situations is so well recognized at this time that police hostage negotiators no longer view it as unusual. In fact, it is often encouraged in crime situations as it improves the chances for survival of the hostages. On the down side, it also assures that the hostages experiencing "Stockholm Syndrome" will not be very cooperative during rescue or criminal prosecution. Local law enforcement personnel have long recognized this syndrome with battered women who fail to press charges, bail their battering husband/boyfriend out of jail, and even physically attack police officers when they arrive to rescue them from a violent assault". [xviii]

I would add patriarchal systems to that list too!

This syndrome is reinforced by internalized beliefs such as "a perceived threat to your survival and a belief that the perpetrator is capable of carrying out this threat. For instance, the abuser may have spoken about things he had done to others, or the victim may have witnessed this happening. An example in the case of an abusive relationship; he may have a story about how a past girlfriend cheated on him, hurt him so much that he just lost the plot and committed a crime of passion. He might relay this story as "she destroyed me" "I loved her" together with "you have come into my life and helped me to love again". This works on a very subtle level to not only let you know that he is very capable of violent crimes of so called "passion", yet it was the ex partners fault. It is also quite flattering that you are the one that saved him from his demon of never being able to love again. You are also now responsible for his welfare. You might even see that wrath in action as he smashes something of yours in a violent fit. The fear here will be that "it could have been you" or it might be you next. He certainly will have a story of past "suffering" and the reason he is like that. A bit like the colonizers of those faraway lands!

We are also led to believe that our cooperation will ensure our loved ones survival. Couple this with evidence of aggression and violence and you might just eventually believe that you need to sacrifice yourself for your loved ones and you are the one that is wrong. Dependent of course on how long the relationship goes on.

Another powerful dynamic in the cycle of abuse is that of the "small kindness" that is seen as a sign of change. When you feel hopeless around the prospect of being able to get away and are trying to stay safe you will probably notice these small signs and interpret them as positive change for the better. So for instance, he brings you chocolates and flowers after a period of abuse and says he is sorry is often such a welcome sign that its significance is usually inflated. He didn't fly into a rage when you burnt the toast; can bring hope that your love is working and he is changing. So when he doesn't abuse you, he gets brownie points!

Isolation from other perspectives will always impact on how your perception grows. The abuser will most probably isolate the victim from people who care about them or can "suss him out". Even if this does not happen entirely the victim will have the experience of trying to keep the abuser happy and walking on eggshells. In these circumstances it becomes easier if you take on the perspective of the one with the power. We become so preoccupied with the world of the ones in power that we lose our own perspective and with nobody to talk to about it, it becomes part of the sanitized myths we live our lives by. This can be so all pervasive that the victim of domestic abuse will often respond angrily to anybody that challenges their perspective in a bid to help them. In lots of cases of domestic abuse, the victim will internalize any retribution towards their abuser as "their fault". So for instance if they call the police and he gets "nicked" it's their fault for calling the police, not his fault for being violent. Of course, the perceived inability to escape compounds this and so the stages of indoctrination are complete.

The final "mental health sickness" diagnosis that <u>is</u> in DSM-5 that is really relevant when linked to the above to show how this is playing out within the bigger picture of "the system and those invisible puppeteers that

Edward Bernays wrote about is:

Hording disorder:

1) Persistent difficulty discarding or parting with possessions, regardless of their actual value.

2) This difficulty is due to a perceived need to save the items and to distress associated with discarding them.

3) The difficulty discarding possessions results in the accumulation of possessions that congest and clutter active living areas and substantially compromises their intended use.

4) The hording causes clinically significant distress or impairment in social or occupational or other important areas of functioning including maintaining a safe environment for self and others.

5) The hording is not attributable to another medical condition i.e. brain injury.

6) The hording is not better explained by the symptoms of another disorder i.e. OCD, delusions etc.

A specification of excessive acquisition: Approximately 80-90% of individuals with hording disorder display excessive acquisition. The most frequent form of acquisition is excessive buying, followed by acquisition of free items. Stealing is less common. Some individuals may deny excessive acquisition when first assessed, yet it may appear later during the course of treatment. Individuals with hording disorder typically experience distress if they are unable to or are prevented from acquiring items.

I would say that was a projection! I am very aware of so called "dysfunctional hoarders"; clutter everywhere! I am also aware of the normality and saner use of this i.e. saving up for a rainy day, but what about, how that becomes a normality in the system where we hoard just for our own family? What about our "Elite"? They do this all the time and they don't _have_ to steal and the stuff their hoard is made of is actually spread out across the world and includes everything we "think" belongs to us too? They have already accumulated, for free, most of the resources on this planet and called it theirs. So in effect whilst they do not steal these things unlawfully, it is actually based on theft from the rest of humanity from long ago.

Another interesting synchronicity that my daughter brought about by telling me that an anti-slave poster in the job centre asks:

"Are you being forced to work for little or no money"?

It also gives a helpline number. Quick as a flash, my daughter asked: "when your children reach the age of three and you must sign on for work and the government makes you go and do work for nothing, can you phone that helpline"?

Hypocrisy at its most insidious!

So! These invisible men who we see as so powerful that we are unable to escape from them or their rules, who we let off so lightly if they give us a little bit of what is already ours by "birthright" on planet earth, who convince us that their perspective is the only perspective and we are inadequate, could just actually be a group of people with power addictions and severe mental health sickness!

A bit like the wizard of Oz when he appeared from behind his curtain! The message is; "it already belongs to us, we do not have to work or die for it, we just think we do" and these invisible men have no power whatsoever to grant us what we seek. Not even if they made "kinder" rules!

The ability to change and transcend belongs to us...

9 SO F**KING WHAT

So what does this goldfish bowl water consist of in our subconscious conditioning? I have discovered plenty of indoctrination created, cultural, racist and sexist beliefs in my psyche and have included some relevant ones in this book. But I think considering just one or two in a bit more depth can help throw some light on how we normalize the myths and how powerful that can be in keeping the system in place.

A really good one to consider and is at the heart of most of our problems is "sex and shame" and the differences in beliefs about men and women within this.

To jump back to Freud; the Oedipus complex, could be a good place to start. This theory grew from his earlier "seduction theory", where he developed the understanding that childhood sexual abuse was the answer to "hysteria" and "obsessional neurosis" (mainly suffered by women). He stated that repressed early memories of molestation were an essential precondition to these disorders. I think he might have had a point there don't you? Especially when you consider that we pass our cr*p on generationally as well. The reason he changed this was simply because, these repressed memories were put together by analyzing and interpreting symptoms and "free associations"[xix] together with "exerting pressure on the patient" to produce such memories. Add that to these molestations not being "consciously" remembered by the patients and his surprise that "all of his patients" produced these abstract memories and he could not comprehend that scale of abuse as probable. It would mean that "all" men were perverse, even his own father! I can see why he might have ended up changing it to; "not having experienced this in reality but having wished that they had" AKA the Oedipus complex. This became the agenda for his work and so therefore a lot of real cases of abuse would be easy to dismiss as "childhood fantasy" even to this very day. He maybe would not have disbelieved it so readily perhaps if he had lived now in these very informative times where child abuse is rife and we are bombarded with examples of historical institutional stuff coming to light and even with prominent figures, like "Jimmy Savile" to name just one among many. This certainly is causing hysteria among the general population at the moment as a parallel to demonstrate how sexual abuse is internalized and there has been a tendency to suddenly start to mistrust everyone. We definitely need to stop that!

Freud developed his psychosexual stages from this concept to "theorize" how children develop. He called them psychosexual because he believed sexual drives and instincts were the things that made humans develop into adults. He reckoned that if we get stuck in certain stages we get problems in adult life. He also believed that life was all about tension and pleasure, the former building up to a crescendo and creating problems with the psyche until it was discharged and that then creates the pleasure. I think Freud got a bit fixated on sex and sexual urges probably because of our crazy culture that views sex as shameful, even sinful and repression of any kind of action, behavior, thought or feeling will always create "f**ked upness". Think about it; If you screwed the lid of a toothpaste tube down tight and exerted enough pressure, the toothpaste would come out where it shouldn't. Well it's the same for all of the above. There is a strange contrast in our society today in that we are surrounded by images and innuendos relating to sex, yet sexual freedom is still something "dirty". You may be very liberal and think it is ok to screw around all over the place, yet these views are not the norm in our society and you will, without a doubt be judged. Think about how we are supposed to get to heaven; purity and virginity are highly valued. Women in the "modern" bible were mainly revered for their virginal state, or they were whores, or they were just "bit players". Celibacy is valued in the church yet we are hearing so many cases nowadays of sexual deviancy and child molestation within our Christian hierarchy that I think that particular toothpaste tube certainly made a great big fat mess once it burst under its own pressure.

Oh man! My mind boggles when I consider the impact this sexual "splitting" has on the human psyche in our sex saturated culture. So once again **what the hell happened to us?**

A really good film to watch on youtube to throw some light on this is "The history of love and sex"[xx]. (I have picked out the main points that were linked to sex as oppression in the video) Terry Jones narrates the history in a light-hearted way but clearly shows that the history of sex and love is also a history of power, politics and religion that has been buried and falsified and shows that Christianity invented sexual repression on a massive scale. This film begins by taking us back to ancient Egypt, where "cosmic sexual activity" was a mainstream belief. In effect sex was how the gods kept the world alive. There was even a myth that a creator god named Atum, masturbated to create the world and to celebrate this on ceremonial occasions, the men masturbated in public.

In this video, Dr Joanne Fletcher (alongside many other Egyptologists and historians, you might want to check out) states that ancient Egypt was built on total balance of opposites and equality between men and women, light and dark, night and day etc was the order of the day. The act of sex was considered as mirroring divine behavior. There is even an early account in the bible of celebration of sex. "The song of songs" sung by orthodox Jews is all about sex and dates back 5000 years, so in fact the joy of sexual love is at the heart of Judaism. Pretty much the same in this as paganism. This is included in the Old Testament, yet we are not told of any "Mrs. God".

There was in fact a "Mrs. God" but she was condemned, thrown out and forgotten in 650 BC; her name was "Ashara" and the Israelites did in fact celebrate sex at the heart of their spiritual beliefs. This was around the same time as the book of "Genesis" was written and the story of Adam and Eve appeared. Women were no longer seen as "life giver" but as "Man's downfall". This view still rears its ugly head to this present day and I have heard quite a few times during my professional career; "Women castrate/de-masculate men with their sexual deviancy and their sharp tongues", not only by men I might add. This is also when "shame" of the body began to develop, brought about by the myth of Eve eating the fruit of good and evil and becoming "Man's" unholy distraction from God! This was also around the same time that military supremacy replaced fertility as a high value.

Terry Jones also spoke of the "band of thieves" who guarded the city of Oedipus. These soldiers were all homosexual and were encouraged to bring their partners to live with them whilst they all defended the city. This ensured that they would never surrender and fight to the death to defend their loved ones (each other). They were so macho that neither of them wanted to be seen as cowardly in the face of danger in front of their lover. In those days sexuality was not used to define a man's courage, that came later.

The birth of Christianity was heralded as a total opposite to paganism and so in order to define itself, it became "anti-sex". Jesus' apostle Paul declared that neither fornicators, adulterers, homosexuals or effeminate men could inherit the kingdom of heaven. He declared unmarried sex to be a sin and advised the widows and unmarried to remain single and celibate. Control of sex was at the heart of a message that sprang from his own warped views and were projected onto and became the morals of the creator god. Before this there was no such thing as a thought or feeling that you needed to be forgiven for, no concept of "sinfulness". By the 4th century AD the church claimed that if you confessed your sins to a priest he would be able to forgive you as an advocate of God. Controlling attitudes towards sex gave the church total power. In effect the message of Adam and Eve, pure love, sinfulness around sexual desire were created to destroy paganism to place Christian priests at the centre of power.

As he correctly states: "the world didn't end so we must now all be sinners".

In Europe more rules were added like "one partner, only one position which was <u>the man on top</u> and it mustn't be enjoyed". A religious leader named John Calvin further stirred the pot by naming the emergence of syphilis as "Gods retribution on sinners". This disease soon spread around the world and created divisions where everyone blamed each other i.e. the English called it the French pox, the Polish called it the German disease, the French called it the Neapolitan disease etc. Women were ultimately blamed for this because of their "sexual appetites" and a man needed to step up the control over their women folk's sinful ways. One problem! Men didn't know what made women tick sexually... In 1559 Renaldus Columbus the Italian medical lecturer, discovered:

"The clitoris"!

I would say just like his name sake he didn't discover it but rather it was more like a massacre (parallel processes again) women were already in possession and knew how it worked. He "discovered" that it was where it was "all at" (for a woman). This need for control over women's sexual urges became antagonized further by the "rise of science". Where science threatened the church within most of the beliefs, it totally upheld and stuck to religious beliefs when considering sex. They related sexual desires in women to "madness"! Now it was not just a sin but a thing that drove you mad. The symptoms were things like; Masturbation, sex after menopause or before marriage and the diagnosis was "nymphomania". In some cases they removed the woman's ovaries in others they removed the clitoris!

In 1760 Artiso, medical advisor to the pope decided that also men who masturbated were driven mad so it was now a medical problem for men too. Too much sex was believed to make you go crazy and many men resorted to castration in an attempt to save themselves. Of course, sexual temptation would be blamed on the woman here too. "Women, castration"? Now where have I heard that one before!

Sex was also seen as a threat to the British Empire in the Victorian era and so lots of discoveries about our pagan roots that were being unearthed around this time depicting sex were hidden from the public's awareness.

The ruling classes thought that if the general public got access to these they might become uncontrollable and it also threatened the established history.

This was carried over into our modern age and in 19th century America laws around sex and the age of consent grew. The age of consent was raised from 10 in the 1880's to 16 by 1889.

Think about it! Rules rarely change desires, in fact they increase them. Think about the pressure on the tube of toothpaste here too. What we are told we can't have, we seem to start desiring, think about the "golden cup"…

These whole messed up contradictory views of the world have created a melting pot of splitting and oppression. Think about our advertising, it is designed to keep us wanting what we can't have. It's the only way that corporations can make money out of sex. If its sinful and immoral or unobtainable i.e. forbidden fruit, the more chance you have of selling it because it is an empire built on guilt.

So! Sex is all around us, it's part of our natural behavior and we are not allowed to have it! No wonder Freud's patients were all seemingly fixated on it, and driven hysterical; guilt, shame and temptation are rife in the fishbowl and have been for many years.

Most if not all of us have been conditioned by the apostle Paul and his perversion thinking followed by lots of others who condemn the act of sex. In lots of cases;

people having an argument and coming to blows in public will not be reported by passersby to the police, yet if a couple were having sex in public, people would probably rush to the phone, morally outraged. We view a beautiful and vital act as dirty, yet we largely condone violence?

If you consider history in depth you will see that attitudes towards sex are ever changing and there is absolutely no such thing as "normal". Any good anthropologist will tell you that there is no such thing as "natural human behavior" it all depends on the environment. The reason children of sexual abuse suffer so much more than children of violence or don't tell anybody is because of the "shame" that is attached and in fact the molestation of children is all about power and control, nothing to do with lust!. If the lid was not screwed down so tight on that tube of toothpaste, it wouldn't come out in the wrong place either would it?

Because sex has been inextricably linked to "power" it has inevitably been warped by perversion and domination of women and the powerless (children or lesser status males). It is used as a weapon of war in the form of rape. It is used to dominate and control in men's prisons, it is being steadily uncovered at the heart of our institutions where child rape and perversions often seem to go hand in hand with power. We have even got a book floating around out there called "50 shades of Gray" that is all about overpowering sex and bondage, "rape of the innocent". Woman all over the planet are reading and enjoying this. Now! I am not a prude, far from it, I don't really care what you do with your sex life. I am just saying, if sexual energy gives us our connection to the universal spirit of creation, and many indigenous shamanic practices include it as important, then it sure is a very big female domination message we are putting into the collective unconscious when we "play rape" during sex isn't it?. Or even in those early days when "man on top" was linked to sex, that one certainly worked didn't it?

When I heard about that book, I felt sick! It was like a stepping up of the control system that most people would deny was happening. If there was one book I would like to erase from our environment it is that one. Although on the other hand it is bringing the subject to light and so therefore it's a good thing.

I am not saying we should all just start being sexually promiscuous and start having sex in the streets etc. I am far too brainwashed to be able to deal with that and so is the rest of the population, I am just showing the madness of what we have become. I don't know what we need to do about that one, I just know it's "f**king us all up" ☺

We could perhaps start by releasing the shame and guilt we feel around sex. Oh yes, and stop with the double standards around men and women. You know, the one that says women who are promiscuous are "slags", yet a man doing the same thing is a hero. I have found during my time as a woman on this planet and especially when working in some depth with women around shame and promiscuity, that most if not all of the women use sex to get closer to a man and often have a stupid idea that a relationship can come from a one night stand. They are usually looking for love and end up getting used, even if they do say (with bravado) that they are using the men. Men on the other hand, tend to be just "thrill seeking" and often run a mile from a woman that puts out on the 1st or even 2nd and 3rd date.

The definition of slag taken from the urban dictionary is:

"Slag: An individual who cares not for relationships beyond the realm of the sexual, these people sleep with many partners not caring about anything save for the moment of climax".

So just remind me; who's the slag then?

Another one of our warped cultural beliefs is that of the image of the witch. Most of our fairy stories and myths will depict her as a "wicked old crone", evil, child eater etc. She is linked to many curses, having sex with the devil and blamed for bringing pestilence and plague. She was blamed for the failure of crops and children going missing in days gone by. She is still in this role today!

In my own "fantasy" world after reading the book by Doreen virtue "Earth angels" and discovering that I fit into the realm of "the wise ones", I had fun in my daydreams having been a "wizard" in another realm and coming back to help heal the Earth. You know, answering the clarion call and all that ☺ I just couldn't associate with being "a witch". It had to be a wizard! I associate the role with such figures as "Merlin" or "Gandalf"; magical, mysterious, funny, powerful, all knowing, all seeing, adventurous, kind, just etc. Yet I viewed the "witch" in the same way as the stories and myths told me to and denied the history of women.

Internalized sexism at its most powerful!

What about that other contentious issue; "swearing"? I found the following piece of info in an article on the web "9 things you probably didn't know about swear words:

[xxi]*People in the "rising middle class" use less profanity.*

"Bourgeois people" typically swear the least, Mohr says. "This goes back to the Victorian era idea that you get control over your language and your deportment, which indicates that you are a proper, good person and this is a sign of your morality and awareness of social rules," she explains. The upper classes, she says, have been shown to swear more, however: while "social strivers" mind their tongues, aristocrats have a secure position in society, so they can say whatever they want — and may even make a show of doing so".

I can't help shaking my head in self righteous despair when I hear people calling swear words "abusive" or "disrespectful", to whom? The upper classes? They don't seem to think it is. Why have we got to pretend to be "less worthy of social comfort than them"? Abusive? What about if I am laughing about something I have done and say; "oh f*f**k sake, I need to sort it out" ☺ How is that abusive? I often wonder how a word can be seen as bad. I mean, If I said to you; "get out of my sight

I think you are a horrible little person" I would see that as abusive. If I just said "f**k it", I am just exclaiming my own act of letting things go. Nothing abusive about that whatsoever, swearing as "wrong" is a very weird belief to have.

I remember during a conversation at work, a colleague said of another member of staff; "I don't swear in front of her out of respect because I know she doesn't like it and it upsets her". He was right about it upsetting her, apparently I think she used to throw a "damsel in distress" fit. When I told him I don't either but not out of respect but through fear of her getting me into trouble". He looked at me very quizzically when I said; "it is a form of oppression". He really couldn't get it when I said; "I don't demand that she must use swear words when she is with me do I"? If I swear by accident I am in big sh*t, if she doesn't swear around me, I am not going to get her into trouble am I? So she can be free to do what's normal in her cultural beliefs and I must change mine? I often laughingly call it; "cultural genocide". In fact in some circles, if you don't swear you are often seen as a bit "stuck up" or "judgmental" and often they feel the need to be wary of you, untrustworthy in fact. Relating this to the above point about being in the "rising classes" I would say that with all that I understand about what type of behaviors can manifest from this role, I probably wouldn't trust them either, as in the above example. Not people who just "don't swear" but people who "judge swearing". I am fine with you not wanting to swear, it's your life I am not always so fine about you judging me for swearing, that's all...

Students of counseling absolutely must, get past this value judgment! It puts added pressure on clients when they are trying to tell you about their life and they are also holding back on their normal way of expressing themselves if they feel you are not accepting of it. It is totally against the code of ethics for promoting healthy relationships (AKA saving the human race) to impose your values onto somebody else or to be judgmental. Unconditional positive regard is definitely a thing that is sadly missing on this planet, including in me. I have to work on it just like the rest of us.

Swearing is also a form of "stress relief", I would rather say "f**k it" than simmer inside (with whatever emotion) trying to hide my feelings. As with most other things and "me", if I am told not to do something, I just sometimes can't help it! I can always tell if there is somebody in my vicinity who doesn't like swearing, I just keep swearing more than usual even without my rebellious side being ignited. It just keeps slipping out! It might be a personality fault in your view, it might be that you judge people who swear as "illiterate" and lacking language skills, but in fact the opposite is true. Stephen Fry talks very eloquently on the subject and I can talk for myself here as well as many students and clients; swearing breaks down social barriers and is a great leveler. Unless of course, you have issues with swearing that is, and then that really is "your stuff", you my friend are the proverbial "fly in the ointment" you might just want to have a look at that!

As with any other form of communication, swear words can be used abusively and that is a different thing, but this is about intent and tone, nothing to do with the actual word. I have been in many circles where calling each other a "c*nt" is a term of endearment...

Stephen Fry made a great point when he said that swear words mainly have sexual connotations and this is why we are "offended" (obviously connected to sex and shame) Yet words like "torture" and "genocide" that refer to horrendous acts that really we ought to be ashamed of are acceptable!

A very fucked up bunch of t*rturous beings we are for sure!

So you see, there are many ways that we have been indoctrinated into believing that our own culture is; "the way we should all be and everybody else must conform to that or be judged as wrong". We just don't very often have cause to analyze our own beliefs in more depth and anyway; if you were brainwashed how would you know?

10 MATRIARCHY?

A re-discovery of self and ancient pre-history is vital if we are ever going to let go of all of our limiting beliefs about ourselves. We have long been told that civilization and "mans evolution" has been built on "survival of the fittest" i.e. competition, yet nature tells a very different story, one of co-operation and togetherness. The animals and the plant life seem to understand this dynamic far better than we do and are far more civil towards each other than we are, they understand that their own survival depends on all the other species, excepting humans nowadays though. We have been spoon-fed a history of battling with the elements and subjugation of nature. Early history of "man's" quest for dominance has been warped and rewritten as a glorious quest for survival and spread to the masses as fact. Little is said about our past before so called "civilization" and so it goes unquestioned that "patriarchy" is human nature.

There is some great stuff on youtube by historian Gwynne Dyer about militarization and the history of war and patriarchy. In one of his videos[xxii] he raises some interesting points, for instance; Archaeologists tend to uncover 100 female fertility figures to every one male figure. Fertility was the key to survival and was traditionally female magic. He states that there was not any oppression of males during matriarchy; rather they just began to feel unimportant when settling down in villages. Early patriarchy started several thousand years ago in many places across the planet; Egypt, Mesopotamia, China, Mesoamerica etc to change the way we lived and built the world we know today.

A female professor of medieval history of Islam Huda Lutfi[xxiii] from the American university of Cairo states that because all of the surviving records are written by men about men, the best way to discover what women were doing in matriarchal Mesopotamia is by considering what the men were now ruling against i.e. walking around the public baths in the nude and expressing matriarchy via their fertility and sexuality. Patriarchy and the emergence of "the state" put an end to humans "fitting in" with nature at this time and began to subjugate pretty much everything; this "new way" could only happen through terror. Symbolism of soldiers and the horrific consequences of going against the rules started to spring up everywhere in the early kingdoms and as Gwynne Dyer aptly states: Absolute power corrupts absolutely! There was no need to put soldiers everywhere to control and subjugate the masses; you just had to put reminders of what could happen to them if they do not obey. Much the same as our world today only we have a much more efficient way of accomplishing this now via the media. I mean, what would you do if you had just watched a woman and her children being tortured and brutally slain for not agreeing to the rules? Would you stand so firmly behind your conviction if you wanted to protect your own children? What about how you might teach those children so that they can survive as adults. It doesn't matter how much you want your old way to stay in place, even if you teach them how to protect themselves whilst whispering to them of the truth, eventually the environment will help wash away the memory. Within a few generations, the reality gets lost, the truth becomes a myth and the new way becomes part of the new version of history. This is the essence of trauma based mind control and it happens all over our planet on different levels to this very day. We have all been traumatized to some extent and the victor's history massively forced on our normality of today through generational mind control and the forgetting that this eventually creates.

One example of a time when women were revered remains in the Shawnee beliefs of the female creator; Grandmother Kuhkoomtheyna.

[xxiv]According to Shawnee mythology, Our Grandmother descended from the world above (Sky World) and created the basis or the foundation of the earth, the turtle. Our Grandmother shaped the world, all bodies of water and tracts of land, and rested her newly created world on the back of the turtle. Our Grandmother performed most of the cosmic creations. At this same time she, with her grandson Cloud Boy and their little dog, rested on the earth

Though some disagreement has occurred among scholars, recently interviewed Shawnee informants maintain, "Our Grandmother has been consistently worshipped as the Divine Being and Great Spirit since our time began" (Standing Bear, 2000).

Now that one is very different to the stuff we are often

fed about God being a man isn't it? Denial of or even denigration of female deities still shapes our culture today. Often when somebody is talking to me about the concept of god and calling it a 'he' and I reply; "my god is a woman", I get the reply; "god doesn't have a gender"! I always reply to this one; "unless it's male eh"? You see "goddesses are often feared among religious people" they see them as the same as this powerful vengeful male god they have created. They see matriarchy as the same as patriarchy in that a "female ruler" would be worse than a male or even the same. I can see the problem here in that I wouldn't go to live in somebody's house if I had treated them badly when they lived in mine either would you? But the concept of matriarchy is different to patriarchy; the female energy supports the masculine and doesn't cut it off, it is not about hierarchy but about equality. There are many people who try to deny that matriarchy ever existed and lots of them are women! A very powerful form of internalized sexism that! How the f**k do they know? There is so much evidence to support the so called "myth" of matriarchy being probable and none whatsoever to support the existence of patriarchy pre-historically! It is generational brainwashing you see...

If patriarchy had been in existence from the start, human beings would all be extinct by now and I wouldn't be writing this book and you wouldn't be reading it. Patriarchy has brought us to the brink of destruction within 5 to 7 thousand years. Highly advanced humans have been on this earth for much, much longer than that.

Our system only manages to continue in its destructive form based on old matriarchal cultural practices of gift giving from pre-history still being upheld by women, we developed this ability to give and give from somewhere didn't we? It definitely wasn't a product of patriarchy which is nowadays seeing women take on an overload of masculine type energy to survive and being a great gift giver was not created by patriarchal rules! It is a product of the natural act of childbirth and very, very difficult to develop and keep alive within a patriarchal split. This environment is why we shut our feelings down not the reason we open them up or keep them alive.

There is a great article on the internet called "[xxv]Gift Giving as the Female Principle vs. Patriarchal Capitalism" by Genevieve Vaughan. She writes about the female principle of gift giving as the human norm and argues that the reason for devaluing female identity is economic. She makes a very stark distinction between gift giving and exchange cultures. She states that the psychological root of woman based economy is the necessity of mothering children for free and the masculine exchange culture came from the devaluing of the feminine and males wanting to be different. A bit like rise of Christianity over paganism and the creation of the "man box". This has created a pattern of devaluation of the mother principle and an over valuing of masculine characteristics like competition, domination and rationalization. Remember, nature doesn't do this and as we are unarguably a part of nature, neither should we!

She writes:

"Scarcity is required for the continuing triumph of exchange over gift giving because if everyone had enough no one would be required or motivated to exchange, and gift giving would be easy. Instead in scarcity, gift giving is difficult, even self sacrificial, and exchange becomes necessary for survival. Accumulation of wealth in the hands of the few serves the creation of scarcity and the hegemony of the exchange paradigm. Accumulation also serves to provide the means for the domination of some over others, those who have more can dominate over those who have less, a process which rewards the dominators whose ego orientation has been constructed and validated by exchange".

It is a very insightful article that highlights the fact that women do most of the important work that underpins the capitalist system for free and is in fact a workable 'woman based economy' that is made difficult by the fact that it is dominated by the masculine based exchange culture. If we took this exchange dynamic out of the picture, the gift giving economy that is already in place will once again thrive. Remember there is much evidence of gift giving economies that thrived in relative peace and harmony before European conquest of the "new world". She puts forward a view of the circle of destruction of patriarchal parasites feeding off the gifts of the many and a model of change that I believe has every chance of success.

"The situation in which we live is dangerous for life on earth because we are paradoxically giving gifts to the exchange paradigm to help the destruction of gift giving and the appropriation of gifts of the many by the few, depriving the many of their inheritance from Mother Nature and Mother Culture.

What can we do?

Step 1. Realize a common (women's) perspective comes from an economic way. Validate that way as the norm. I believe it has been cancelled from many different disciplines, made invisible, disqualified and devalued. It can be restored to view. For example I have developed a theory of language as gift giving.

2. Realize men have been socialized in to a psycho-economic way, and identify what that economic way is in contrast to gift giving. After investigating it for a long time I have come to the conclusion that exchange economics is artificial and self similar to the socialization into male gender.

3. Bring back men (and women) to the economic way of the Mother, abolishing 'economics'.

4. Let humanity flower according to gift giving, having found a dynamic which PRODUCES the human characteristics, of language, nurturing, sociality, relationship. So we will create and find our common human identity by dismantling an artificial dominant identity, an achievement which will liberate gift giving and the nurturing identity from the host position at the same time that it dismantles the parasite position".

There is strong evidence of matriarchy that has been uncovered dating right back to Paleolithic times. This is summed up really well in another youtube video

entitled; "[xxvi]The secrets of the stone age". This film throws a different perspective on our ancient roots embedded in the ice age. Looking at these clues through different lenses other than patriarchal, it is clear to see that the beginnings of architecture, medicine and writing attributable to "civilization" was actually present in Paleolithic times and did not suddenly appear in later cultures. Some 20,000 years before humans settled into villages, during the last ice age, there is evidence of humans living in harmony with nature. This gets written off in the patriarchal perspective as "primitive" rather than a high level of intelligence that is needed to coexist with nature. Yet they were our social and intellectual equals. They had to be highly intelligent to be able to survive let alone thrive in icy barren landscapes. They lived in groups that regularly met up with other groups to give gifts and exchange ideas. The reason we have been so misinformed about our ancient past is because we have only been told half the story, the half that concentrates on what men were doing. If we look at what the women were doing we find all the evidence we need of ancient intelligence. Women were the main food providers, they gathered nuts, fruit, vegetables and small animals. They needed to have a vast understanding of their environment to do this. These people were healthy and strong. We have only been told about early macho man hunting and killing woolly mammoths and this view has more to do with masculine ego and male archaeologists who studied it than it has to do with the truth as J.M. Adovasio (archaeologist) puts it. He also said; "who's going to risk standing beside an elephant and trying to kill it with non gunpowder projectiles"? It's an incredibly risky business and besides only 20% of the Paleolithic diet was meat. These people were robustly healthy and lived long lives which produced "Grandmothers" who looked after the children and passed on the knowledge of the landscape. This freed up the younger women who played active roles and were at the heart of society. They created and run highly productive and skilled trading cultures and there is much evidence of standardized production of ivory beads and ceramics. There was also a highly advanced understanding of textile technology and they produced and wore fine cloths and braided their hair in a highly sophisticated way. There are many Venus figurines from this period that male archaeologist thought were fetish figures made by men for men (male ego again) but these could just as likely have been made by women to teach of the mysteries of woman hood. There is no way of telling but we did after all survive and if we had been patriarchal and everything done by men with women being objectified this would not have happened. Think about it, this was a barren and hostile natural ice age environment where fighting each other and killing mammoths to survive would have led to sure and certain extinction.

There are underground caves in France and Spain that were not used as "homes" or even ancient "art galleries" as we have been led to believe. Rather they were highly elaborate systems of tunnels that you need to crawl through that symbolize the birth process. The journey was as important as the arrival. Ceremonial centers at the end of these tunnels are decorated with amazing works of art depicting the seasons through the animals that were precise and even painted around corners with perfect proportion. You cannot see the whole image unless you walk around it and that takes astonishing skill. The ability evident in these caves was not thought to exist in the "modern world" until the renaissance period once men had mastered it. When visiting these caves, Picasso said: "We have invented nothing". These caves are much more likely to have been used as ceremonial centers of communion with the animal spirits of nature, they were also either painted by women or children because of the intricacy of the finger painted designs made by small hands.

This knowledge is often dismissed by anti-feminist writers who can see no further than the things they are perceiving within their own established mind set and it is true that on its own could not really be used as "proof positive" but neither can their views that men have always been in charge and that is human nature! It's a good job that's not true because like I said, we would have killed ourselves off many thousands of years ago if there had never been a balance between the sexes. It is a fact that nature will always overcome anything that is not in balance with the universal law of cooperation and harmony. If it can't cooperate it is eventually shown the door!

If it is not the case that we came from gift giving and matriarchy, and I do not believe that for one moment, then it might be a good idea to give it a try now. After all, patriarchy and capitalism will lead us all off of the cliff together relatively soon, so we have nothing to lose! Anyway, to deny there ever was a matriarchy and to claim this as a "new idea" would surely be doing a disservice the many cultures that have gone before us and lived peacefully side by side like in the Americas.

There is still more to uncover I think. I was once of the opinion that we knew everything about our history and there was nothing left to discover. I was entirely wrong about that and evidence is emerging nowadays of not only the pyramids and the sphinx being many, many thousands of years older than we are led to believe, but also ancient sites all over the world that would have taken incredible technology, machine tools of some kind and skill to create that are thousands of years old. We cannot reproduce these enormous fetes of engineering with our technology today so how is it that these structures were believed to be around when we were allegedly living in caves?

A theory I am kind of researching and playing around with at the moment is based around the "ancient knowledge" or "myth" whatever the case may be of "the collapse of a highly advanced civilization on Earth that disappeared with a cataclysm that brought on the ice age. Think about it, who would be the most likely ones to survive a cataclysm today? The native populations that are still connected to the natural world that's who (and this would lead future discoverers to believe in "cave people"), the rest of us would more likely be f**ked! No technology, no shops, no piped energy, no transport, no tools. How many of us have the skills to survive this? How many of us know how to live in nature? What would happen to our paltry little structures over thousands of years? We would need to build earthquake proof structures that were large enough to withstand the erosion of time, something like the pyramids; to let future generations know of our existence. The rest of it would just disappear from whence it came. So I wonder if evolution is cyclical, everything else is, so why not evolution?

11 DISCOVERING THE PLANETARY SCRIPT

The thing that sparked a deeper exploration of my own indoctrination regarding "witches" was another film on youtube called "Burning times" that I discovered whilst researching women's history or "herstory". I had kind of missed the "witch connection" to women and oppression, mainly because I had not taken the re-emergence of "Wicca" very seriously and it had caused a block. True, I had a bit of internalized sexism going on here in that "witch magic" was a bit too cranky for me, but I also saw it as a bit "cultish" you know, all of us must believe this or that and prance around dressed up like fairy story figures waving fake magic wands and following a bloke named Aleister Crowley. Whilst another bloke named Gerald Gardner "created" Wicca, he took his ideas from Aleister Crowley's beliefs that came from; Freemasonry, Egyptian ideologies and Celtic law. Gerald Gardeners "Book of shadows" and all of the ceremonies and rituals were based on Aleister Crowley's work. Even the one law "do what you will, may you harm none" came from Crowley.

I didn't know much about either of them except that they were both freemasons, still don't, about as much as I know about Wicca or any other organized belief system, I just can't sort out the wheat from the chaff and all of the systems of belief were developed from earlier teachings and would have been tarnished by the patriarchal perspective, so I can't really comment further than that. I do know that putting things in boxes creates separation so to me the rules and belief systems may or may not have held merit but I prefer to work out "spirituality" through trial and error so therefore do not allow myself to buy into any concept in its entirety. I research things to find if other people are saying or have said anything that helps my own understanding of the issues that are my focus of the moment. I had not had any cause really other than a mild interest i.e. to consider "spell magic" with "affirmations and decrees" etc to look into Wicca. It is always worth considering the beliefs of any organized system but I don't commit myself to one way and so therefore had totally ignored the history of "witches and women" because of my own internalization of negative images and the patriarchal slant.

I was however committed to discovering "herstory" and as the witch trials, I have since discovered, were mainly "herstory" it was a subject I was destined to explore.

It was another split!

The essence of "herstory" is captured well in the film and I have researched different points further and before on my long and lonely path. (I have tried to capture the main essence and sequence of this film whilst adding further points of my own and others) This film states that when the Romans came to Britain they did not destroy the religious practices of the people. In fact they joined in with some of them, whilst also renaming them and beginning the destruction of others of course. I suspect that maybe this film is a little too kind to the Romans though or perhaps I misinterpreted the meaning. There was evidence of rape and mass destruction by the Romans and much evidence that temples, towns and cities were destroyed. There is also some quite telling information in the writings of the Romans themselves although they need to be taken with a pinch of salt because they were after all the "victors" and came from a vastly different culture so their perceptions would have been tarnished. For instance:

[xxvii]*We British are used to women commanders in war; I am descended from mighty men! But I am not fighting for my kingdom and wealth now. I am fighting as an ordinary person for my lost freedom, my bruised body, and my outraged daughters.... Consider how many of you are fighting — and why! Then you will win this battle, or perish. That is what I, a woman, plan to do! — let the men live in slavery if they will.*

This was a statement said to have been made by Boudicca which raises questions (for me) like; how long had it taken the soldiers to enslave these people? How come they had managed to do that with the amount of men that Boudicca's tribe eventually managed to overcome? The Natives must have been a bit of a push over mustn't they? This woman was fighting for freedom; and slavery takes time to establish. How come she got so many people to rise up because of rape? Rape is a weapon and a product of war, so how come they were so outraged if they were warlike themselves? The Romans felt great shame at being beaten by a woman; they were referring to Boudicca who had raised an army after her daughters had been raped by the soldiers and she was tortured. This type of statement about women was a common thing in the early Roman records and another one clearly showed their perceived superiority over women:

"[xxviii]Boudicca, a Briton woman of the royal family and possessed of greater intelligence than often belongs to women".

Whilst this invasion eventually led to a total destruction of our so called 'pagan' practices, values and beliefs it makes sense that these continued on past this invasion connected to my own knowledge of the process of human change. These values and beliefs were kept alive for centuries in an ever decreasing circle that culminated in them either being turned into a "myth" practiced by primitive people who knew nothing and so were heathen "evil" beliefs or assimilated into the newly developing indoctrination of the Christian conquerors. A pattern that is evident among all historic invasions of "virgin territory".
Women continued their ancient practices and traditions and were still "folk" leaders, counselors, visionaries and healers i.e. "wise ones". Around the 15th century this developing destruction of the native beliefs came to a head and women were branded as "witches" and worshippers of the devil. So the wise women, healers at the edge of social change were confused with "Satanists" and it is still embedded in our unconscious

belief system to this very day. It was during the birth of the renaissance period that the witch craze flourished and women's power became associated with darkness and death. For instance in our modern day we celebrate Halloween and create images of "evil wicked witches" on a day that was once called 'samhain' and was a time to remember the ancestors. Europeans lived closely with their ancestors too just like the peoples of the Americas. It is also interesting that the renaissance period was when "men's mastery of art" was discovered, you know the one that had been present during the Paleolithic period.

There was a time in Europe too that older women were revered, the conical hat was seen as a sign of wisdom, the cauldron as the vessel which creates the magical healing power. Their wisdom came about through years of experience that culminated in "wrinkles" that were also desirable. The women were the nutritionists, the healers, the midwives; and so the cauldron would have been used to create health and life. This change in perceptions came about over a few hundred years powered by the propaganda campaign of "women's power as evil" and is still firmly stuck in our subconscious conditioning today as we associate "witch with evil". Witchcraft was a cultural tradition around the world, Anthropologist Margaret Alice Murray wrote about what she called "The witch cult in Western Europe" and states in the book of the same name:

"The mass of existing material on this subject is so great that I have not attempted to make a survey of the whole of European

witchcraft but have confined myself to an intensive study of the cult in Great Britain. The cult appears to have been the same throughout Western Europe".

I think the word "cult" is rather misleading here but she does in fact show us that connection to the earth and natural, diversity was in practice across Europe before patriarchy descended. So it was not only the indigenous tribes that we found in far flung places that revered "Earth, our Mother" we too have our roots in peace, reverence of diversity and an eternal connection to each other.

This film also speaks of these societies of women healers that can still be found practicing their healing arts today across the globe and are nowadays called "witch doctors" I called them this in my journal excerpt included earlier in this book on page **(67)**. Modern medicine rejected these beliefs for many years and is only now beginning to re-examine them. In order to survive and protect themselves whilst keeping the natural beliefs alive Christian symbolism and meanings were added to the healing ceremonies but the healing was and still is about the ancient natural practices of the "old ways" and nothing to do with the religious slant.

A Dominican Father of a Catholic Church college in California, Mathew fox, spoke out in this film about the "hate mail" that he received from "good Christians" regarding having a "witch" on the college faculty. This "Witch" was a woman named Miriam Simos who later called herself "Starhawk" and had emerged from a birth family of Russian Jewish immigrants to become a leading voice in the re-emergence of the "spirituality of women" and actually has a master's degree in feminist therapy. She worked in various colleges and lectured on the art of ritual to; therapists, spiritual "seekers" and even clergy. Mathew Fox stated that he thought the "witch burning" was over until he read some of those hate mail letters that wished his fate to be one of "burning in hell" because he had her on his campus. So you see, some part of these people's subconscious programming deemed that condemning others to horrendous torture in the flames of hell was justifiable because of a belief!

In days gone by this newly emerging spiritual cult of Christianity spread the message throughout Europe via gigantic symbols of the cross and horrific public executions by fire and other painful torturous means and because of this, millions lost their lives in an orgy of mass destruction of a nature based way of life that resulted in trauma based mind control that was eventually forgotten. There are no memorials to these people, very little memory exists and so it shows us how rapidly trauma based mind control works in getting people to forget. This thing that we have largely forgotten became known as the "Inquisition" and in 16th century the "Witch hunts" were the mainstream norm. Many generations of children watched as their mothers were burnt at the stake. Many people argue that the "witch hunts" were not about the destruction of women by citing the fact that some of the witches burnt at the stake were men. This is very true but about 85% were women and the whole thing was a destruction of "feminine energy based" spirituality so therefore in its highest meaning it was all about destruction and subjugation of the feminine principle and as women are equipped to carry that wisdom best it was a female focused genocide. The film identifies it as a "woman's holocaust" and states that whilst there are varying beliefs on how many were killed the highest number is of 9 million over a period of 300 years. There is as much confusion over the numbers in this event as there is in the other event that was happening around about the same time in the Americas or any other event in our patriarchal history. We must remember that a lot of "herstory" was destroyed when writing "history" and so numbers are probably never going to be agreed upon but there are many books on the subject that hold the information like Margaret Alice Murray's works or perhaps; "Witchcraze a new history of the European witch hunts" by Anne Llewellyn Barstow among others that are really worth exploring. Old nature based ways were burnt along with the witches and a way of life was destroyed a way that saw women and men working alongside each other and connected to their environment in harmony and not subjugation. The goddess traditions such as; women dancers and the queen of the May leading the mayday celebrations, were increasingly practiced by men and turned into "quaint" carnivals that remember a time of magic through patriarchal eyes. These early people lived in harmony with the land, the seasons, the cosmos and their immediate environment. Their values, beliefs and customs were developed with relevance to their particular environment and so there would have been no negating of other beliefs and practices, no "My god is better than your god" crap; with people from other environments. Pretty similar to the vast expanse of land known as "the Americas" and the civilizations that were there before the Europeans. During the renaissance period in Europe there were two belief systems running along side by side; the religion of the elite (controlling power) and that of the ancient people of the land. Christianity established its "standardization" of doctrine by turning goddesses into saints so therefore demoting them. The Christian religion still has one of these converted goddesses in Mary and she is still known to this day by her old pagan titles of "Mother of god the queen of heaven". The patriarchal religion of the elite retained power whilst the goddess cultures were driven to annihilation. You see, direct ability to connect to spirit through the earth, sky and water were a dangerous threat to the power of the catholic priests. If you can talk to god yourself then they are pretty much redundant so they quashed dissent and made more rules which ultimately came out in f*cked up ways (remember the toothpaste). Women had to be desecrated for this to happen because they were the healers, the counselors and the wise ones and this quite obviously had political implications on a governmental system that was inextricably linked to Christianity in its many guises. Crazy, crazy stuff was happening like midwives being accused of going against gods will by easing the pain of childbirth that was said to be a punishment from god for their lustful ways. Rules were put in place that stated nobody must cure or offer healing services unless they had a "qualification" and as women were not allowed to study and nobody from the natural world would be able to get very far either, this gave the government total power and birthed the male medical profession and I feel, the potential beginnings of the desire to go to school, among the saner people who lived in the natural way. During the "witch trials" it was the testimony of male doctors that sent women to their deaths and their aim was seemingly to take control of women's sexuality and reproductive abilities. We do after all need lots of soldiers to keep the establishment safe don't we?

Trade also expanded around this time and land acquisition began to develop its genocidal fingers across Europe. Many of the natural people were forced off their homelands in similar fashion to the requerimiento carried out in the Americas. The gathering of groups became branded as "plotting against men and/or the state" and so the destruction of the community had really taken hold. Public executions were carried out to reinforce the idea that "gathering in groups was illegal" and trauma based mind control worked just as well then as it does today. Husbands were advised to beat their wives from the Christian pulpits and women branded the root of all evil. Sexuality in women was seen as a block to mans holiness and Saint Thomas Aquinas was recorded as saying:

"One of the greatest pleasures we can look forward to when we get to heaven is watching the tortures of the eternally damned" …. F*ck! A psychopathic lunatic! A bit like President Theodore Roosevelt (who was awarded a Nobel peace prize) when speaking of the unprovoked raid on an Indian settlement in Colorado in the late 19th century that was planned for a time when only the old men, women and children were present. The Indians waved to greet them, the soldiers then massacred them in horrific ways that we still have records of and came from the recollections of the soldiers involved. They were horrifically exterminated. This was described by this President Roosevelt, this Nobel peace prize winner as:

"As righteous and beneficial a deed as ever took place on the frontiers of America"!

Running alongside this growing fear of women and culminating into an explosion slightly earlier during the 14th century a period of 200 years of plagues and epidemics that were increasingly blamed on "women's magic" engulfed Europe. This added to the growing suspicion of women especially as the population of women began to outnumber men, and so much death and destruction of all kinds marked the explosion of the mainstream mechanism that we live in today. This decrease in the male population was probably caused by the increase of wars and women being more resistant to the diseases. Because of this women could not always find husbands and many became independent by the 16th century and so the denigration of widows and old women became even more important to the oppression of powerful women and the continuation of the patriarchal state. Where once wrinkles were revered, they were now feared! The "witch persecution" was an answer to the Christian institution that was feeling threatened as their "new way" wasn't working and so the need to tell stories about witches and their danger to the public became a way to take the pressure off of the established rulers. So it wasn't the pope, the church or the state that was causing the problems but the witch! She became the hag, the devils agent, the sexually insane, the seductress, the temptress, the evil force and "man's downfall". Although witches who were burnt were not all old, not all female and some of them were even children, the image of the "hag" has been internalized and feared as in our present day fear of wrinkles and the flourishing industry we have developed to get rid of them. Hag used to mean "Woman with sacred knowledge" it was once great to be an old woman believe it or not!

The witch hunts became big business during the developing exchange economy everything had to be paid for and many professions developed out of this frenzy of masculine zeal. There was a huge profit ethic where bookkeepers, jailers, hunters, lawyers, and professions of all kinds charged for everything connected to their services in eradicating witches. An entire economy had sprung up from the subjugation of female magic and with all of the fear and scuffle for resources; people suspected and began to target each other. There were monetary gains for handing in witches, a bit like our government of the moment who blames unemployment on the unemployed and asks people to grass each other up for 50 quid!

The [xxix]Malleus Maleficarum; *Latin* for "The Hammer of Witches" is an interesting book to read that makes apparent the huge misogynistic focus of the times. This book was used by witch hunters across Europe and was widespread because of the invention of the printing press that occurred around the same time. Suspected witches were tortured to gain a confession and to get her to name others. She was tortured up to 3 times and she always confessed by the 3rd. This is where the saying "The third degree" comes from. There are many records of these executions probably mainly because of the financial weight that was attached yet there is only one surviving letter from a woman awaiting execution as a witch:

"Oh husband, they take me from thee by force. How can god suffer it, my heart is broken and my children are orphaned. Bring me something that I can take my own life and not get tortured so I can die with less pain".

This hammer of witches was hugely focused on the fear of sex and women. It was a feast of projections and repression and was commissioned by Pope Innocent 8th.. Even the title is focused on the feminine "Malefica" and not the more inclusive masculine "Maleficus". Pretty much like when the bible refers to "man" it means all of us, yet "woman" means exactly what it says on the tin! Women and nature based values and practices were buried and/or rewritten and we really would do ourselves a favor if we turned our perceptions around, we might just turn the fate of the human race around along with it.

This is definitely a theme I had planned to rewrite my script around to help me move forward in my own life so you can imagine my delight when I was searching the origins of my surname and found a Witch connection! This research had not been sparked by the witch thing and I was also of the opinion that I had been given to the wrong family at birth so had not really become interested in their genealogy. The search was driven by a memory when considering the spiritual messages given to me in the past and connected to all sorts of things like astrology, indigenous herstory, nick names, numerology and memories that stick in my mind etc. I remembered that many years ago whilst in Cornwall I had come across the heraldic coat of arms and meanings for both mine and my children's father's surnames. His grew from "The defenders of the church" and mine from "attackers of the church"! I didn't find out much more about this and the paperwork that came with the heraldic exploration has long since disappeared into the mists of time. However the stark contrast of opposites and the upside down view of this in our relationship that turned out to actually be spot on considering all I have learned since, had come back to me whilst recalling these messages from the past and what they were telling me about who I am. So I decided to Google it! Low and behold I discovered that "Brewsters" were the female brewers of those times when women were healers and in order for the establishment to commandeer the developing mass production of alcohol, these female brewers were branded as "witches" and much of the symbolism around the witch today came from the symbols connected to the female brewers like the cats, pointed hats, cauldrons and besom broomsticks that resembled ale stakes. They would definitely be seen as attackers of the church and was a projection of the aggressor indeed, who would see themselves as a victim!

"Does Brewster Sara deserve a good ducking[xxx]" is a great article on Brewsters brewery website, and adds to my research of self in ways that touch many areas of my life. For instance the alcohol connection and when hops were introduced the profits increased because of a longer shelf life and men began to turn to the profession of brewing whilst vilifying the female brewer's beer. Questioning the quality, calling her dirty, saying she was a cheat or she kept a disorderly house. Many things I have been accused of in my past I can tell you! So my namesakes were forced out of alcohol and of being independent women, by the drive of economics and the witch craze. This article also goes on to describe the fact that women did all the brewing and much is written about the Brewsters, one famous one being "mother Bunch" who was described as:

"An excellent companion and sociable, she was very pleasant and witty and would tell a tale, let a fart, drink her draught, scratch her arse, and pay her groat as well as any chemist of ale whatsoever"

A woman after me own heart ☺

I often, when asked if I have a spirit name, joke; "yes blows with the wind" because I try to bend and sway with the world whilst staying rooted to source like the willow, rather than try to hold it back like the oak. Sounds very spiritual doesn't it? But I always add; "Actually I birthed this name from the other meaning above". It isn't something I do often, not the farting thing, but the spirit name thing, only if I am asked. I prefer to be known as "Mand" because when people call me that, it lets me know they have accepted me and are easy in my presence. But people can call me what they like as long as it's not abusive and if it is then that's cool too as long as they don't mind taking the name "a**hole" ☺

If you remember from the first book I wrote about the power of re-writing your script and as it is such a focus for me have decided to re-write this planetary script into something of meaning to me.

[xxxi]The power of the pen is mightier than the sword!

12 A DIFFERENT WRINKLE IN TIME

Long, long ago on the beautiful and vast Island of Alma Diosa[xxxii] there lived a long forgotten assortment of tribes of people who were still connected to the spirit of nature and who drew their inspiration from the sea. They understood that we are all connected by water and that it was the holder of all memory. They lived peaceful and happy lives but just lately they had seen visions of a great darkness encroaching from the skies. A vision of a thunderous god who would corrupt and destroy their way of life. There was an unease descending and a sense of impending doom filled the energy all around them. Their rituals of balance and harmony and reverence for all forms of life were beginning to hold less power and so they knew that something big was happening. Something about this darkness stirred their memory, there was something in their past that had been forgotten but nobody knew what it was. They still continued to celebrate differences between cultures, genders and species and all lived in harmony within roles they were drawn to. Nobody was put in a stereotypical role and people knew that the progression through stages of life was a wondrous journey that they had played from many perspectives of culture, gender and species in a never ending string of past and future lives. There were no rules except responsibility for self and others and then "first do no harm". Everybody was productive and valued till the end of their days and beyond. Age was a sign of great achievement and wisdom was measured in wrinkles whilst the wisdom of the journey was revered. There was no need to fight about who did what the best and people just discovered what they and other members of their group were good at. Of course there was not total perfection, they still had skirmishes and disagreements and acted out dramas, but these were usually settled quite quickly and valuable lessons were learned. There was no hierarchy and the cultures were of circles rather than pyramids. There were rituals of magic and song and dance and celebration and abundance. Knowledge was shared and not owned and listening eagerly to each other brought great togetherness. There were great cities and towns and communities of people all living with the knowledge that they depended on each other to survive and be happy. Children were welcomed back into the tribes and remembered from their lifetime before. There were great works of art and technology, great healing methods that are lost to us today that sprang readily from this advanced knowledge that was being brought in with each new birth. They were all connected through invisible energy cords and if one person was either hurt or happy the rest of them felt it. This energy resonated throughout the Isle of Alma Diosa and people developed their own ways of helping to heal themselves and others to retain the balance. Some were good at creating peace and harmony through herbal remedies, some danced and sang, some did incantations and rituals, some were astrologers and some recorded the herstory in a way that re-wrote any pain and suffering into a meaningful concept that could be transmuted through the magic of the pen among many other things. Most of them were good teachers, story tellers and students and enjoyed this steady rhythmic flow of learning. Both sides of their brain was used and when these were in balance it created abilities that are believed to be fanciful today like; telepathy and teleportation, manifestation, levitation, total acceptance and unconditional love.

Then one day this dread that they had been feeling, arrived in its physical manifestation on their shores in the form of half starved soldiers of which they had never before seen the like. These new people were all men and were also not too hot on their personal hygiene either. The natives greeted them as messengers of spirit and they were treated kindly and fed well. They were given gifts in celebration and as a sign that invited them to feel welcome. They knew these were still beautiful souls because they had chosen to incarnate as "Darkness bearing" humans but they could see past this to the shining bright soul connection that the bearer could not feel. These new arrivals were so lost in their left brain that their spiritual connection was intellectualized and not experienced by them. They had silly rules and their over sized left brain made them believe in scarcity and they were displaying symptoms of this imbalance like hording resources and not sharing. In their innocence the Alma Diosans took it back and redistributed it. This made the visitors left brain grow more powerful and the dread became more tangible!

This gradually degenerated into an orgy of patriarchal

abuse with many people of the native cultures reincarnating continually to try to stop the spread of this disease of unbalanced left brain energy and turn it around with their love to help the "stinkers" remember their mother. Alas, over time, the culture of the invaders had begun to infiltrate and traumatize these ancient souls and many began to forget and fell into darkness during their lives as they suffered horrific genocide and abuse. They were watching their fellow humans killing their close family and friends. Their love for the whole of the human race began to shut down and their magic all but stopped working. They turned to alcohol and picked up on the ways of these "stinking soldiers" and their race. There was a universal crisis occurring where it was finally realized that this was the beginning of the end of the golden age that had been prevalent across the planet for a long time. In their comfortable zones they had missed the impact of the years before across the globe that they had been unaware of; an imbalance had developed and it was too late. They had stopped travelling to other lands a few thousand years before because they had noticed the fear in faraway places beginning to develop and it had started to impact on their magic, the darkness in faraway realms had become a little bit scary. They had decided to stay away, build up their energy for a while and check it out later and hope that they would have sorted it out themselves. But it just became part of their culture not to leave the safety of Alma Diosa and they forgot. Now they were slap bang in the middle of the darkness that had made them too scared to shine a light upon it. Right at the height of the downfall many people had been burned at the stake and tortured and many women branded "Witch" or "Chingada" meaning "woman who allows herself to be raped" and was the lowest form of insult. Most of the islander's spiritual practices had been branded as evil and so these began to go underground and held much less magic because the love for humanity was dying and because of the fear. They realized that they were looking at the ghosts of themselves of the future in these soldiers. They recognized the great spiritual beings that were trapped in the grip of the over developed left brain. They also recognized that if something else was not now done to adapt to the changes and keep alive the memory of a peaceful way then they too would become totally like this strange form of humanity that was being sucked dry by a parasitical cult called patriarchy. They were already forgetting the past...

Many souls decided to incarnate away from the tribe to begin the journey back to peace once their civilizations were all but annihilated and the turnaround of the patriarchal hiccup was beginning to gain ground as those brave spiritual warriors that kept choosing to come back as an aggressor were bravely, courageously and magnificently remembering who they were before they were ripped from their mother's bosom...

We jump forward in time to the 20th century which was when the descendants of Alma Diosa could come back. There was a re-emergence of love happening at that time and many new souls with no genetic memory of genocide were also joining the quest for planet Earth. These Alma Diosans were badly wounded souls and so they needed to be reintroduced to family cultures that would make a great cover story for their deep pain whilst they learned how to integrate the messages from the past. Their deep love for humanity supported by the new souls and the bravery of the aggressors who turned towards the light was finally included in the call. Alas some of them were lost in action as their circumstances got out of control and their disconnection from source and blaming of others who their love had allowed them to trust became unbearable. But they quickly reincarnated again with much more caution in choosing their birth circumstances and a memory of how not to try to transcend within the medium of substance abuse, power and addictions.

One of these was a little girl called Mandy who was a very sweet little girl but who also began to develop her mischievous side quite early on. She was often called "stinker" by her father. Her sister who had chosen to reincarnate as a steadying influence for Mandy a couple of years earlier immediately named her "Chinga" in a bid to tell him he was wrong as she still remembered it as a projection of the "stinking soldiers" from another time before this life, this new child was called "Chinga" not "stinker"! This little girl then carried the memory of her past life in her early years through the nickname "Chinga".

She was a very brave little girl and had no fear of the

dark until she started to have recurring dreams around the age of 5. She was in her own house in this dream and was chased up the stairs by a witch in a conical hat and dressed all in black. When she reached the top of the stairs with the witch hot on her heels, she jumped over the balcony in a bid to escape. When she hit the ground she woke up, felt relief and fell back to sleep. She had this dream every night until she finally became very scared of the dark indeed. She also kept getting in trouble a lot and ridiculed by this person who was called a "Father" and a "Mother" that loved her when he wasn't around; but Mandy seemed to become invisible to her when he was. Around this time she developed a word that she said to herself, that always seemed to help when she was under pressure. It had a very "clicky" sound that seemed to clear her throat and reverberate in her soul and she became addicted to it. This word was "Konkchiel" a very strange word indeed" but it helped.

She used to watch films on the TV about "Island cowboys and Alma Diosans". She was very drawn to the Alma Diosans and even though they were scary she used to marvel at their long hair, their way of life and their athletic abilities. She even used to tell people her grandparents were Alma Diosans she was so fascinated by them. She always wanted long hair just like them, but her mum used to cut it regularly and even perm it! God she hated her hair and often made long wigs out of wool that she made into two plaits just like the Alma Diosans.

She was blighted from her very early years by a deep wound, a fear of watching others die. She even used to cry over the animals who lost their lives in films. She felt absolutely horrified at the prospect of remaining alive whilst others die and started a childhood quest to discover what happens to people that do die.

She used to play with the nature spirits in the garden that the people around her called "fairies", when she told people about them and tried to show them, she couldn't see them either because they couldn't. She started to believe she was making things up, never saw them again and forgot about them.

As she got closer to adulthood, the abuse she was suffering at home became horrendous, especially when her sister got married and left. She felt very alone when she watched the behavior of others and wishing they could love each other decided they were all "crazy"! But she also thought that she was the one that was wrong, not only had she not been able to create loving relationships with them but this person she called "dad" was always telling her she was horrible too and "mum" seemed to think he was right.

She decided to escape and made many attempts to run away but always ended up going home. One time she even handed herself in to the police after running so far away that she couldn't get home. She expected to be on the missing persons list and they would know about her. This wasn't actually the case because her parents hadn't even noticed she was missing. She eventually made good her escape by running off with a man that lived in the woods and fields. She found that living outside in nature, cooking and washing over an open fire and living off the land was something she was very good at and she felt at home! Something that blighted this was the presence of extreme abuse and ridicule coming from this man. His hygiene wasn't that hot either, but she felt responsible for him and besides she had 5 little souls in her care that she would be unable to support if she went back into the system she was living outside of.

People in that system supported this man's beliefs anyway and often told him where she was when she ran away! At least that was different; at least someone cared enough to report her missing! It was a small sign but in her accepting self blaming soul it was validation that love was still alive and could conquer all, the "magic" was working!

Once she woke up and realized there was a different way in relationships she decided to run away again. This turned into total chaos and she began to dance and sing, drink and take drugs, it felt like relief, it felt like nothing else mattered and it was fun. The trouble was, the more she danced and made merry, the worse her children's life become. They began to hate her and attack her and she turned more and more to the fake transcendental state of alcohol and other drugs.

She finally reached the bottom of the pit and got zapped by a "wake up" wave of energy that originated unbeknown to her from an "attack on people that were not used to being attacked" on the affluent faraway island of Alma Diosa! She immediately responded to the call by cleaning up her act and getting on with her mission! Her memory had started to re-emerge and long forgotten truths were being presented to her as she moved upwards into the "rising classes" and discovered they were full of crazy people too. People that professed to love, but is in fact "love you only if you fit the right boxes".

She was so caught up in her mission to create more love that she had not had time to "put it all together". Then a very grave and awful thing happened! The father of her children was killed in an accident and there was great sadness and grief for her children who were badly impacted on and had difficult and different demons to battle. She felt utterly helpless and in grief for her children because of the birth cord and huge compassion for the man who's death was only the second she had experienced by a significant person in her life. This led to huge tensions as the divided family were once more flung together and it brought up her own issues with non-forgiveness. She realized that she couldn't help them if they were feeling that she thought he was horrible, they wouldn't be able to cling to her for comfort whilst dealing with their pain. She could remember a time when they had all loved her and she thought that could re-emerge. When it didn't and her children started to divide again, it brought back resentments towards him for how he had divided them. She knew that she had to forgive him and remembered the songs he used to play. Dark and dreary country and western songs that spoke of death and needing a mother to love. She played them with two of her daughters and they all cried together. She felt real forgiveness and could clearly see that whilst he was a powerful negative force in their lives whilst he was alive, he could now be a powerful positive force in bringing them back together. This served as a wakeup call for her and she developed the idealistic belief that they could all run off together into the sunset. She had forgotten the journey is all about mountains and valleys and anything that happens overnight is just not destined to last.

She had started to realize that as she was talking about him to them in forgiving ways, they had started to see him as saint and her as sinner! Sh*t! Now she had more reasons to test her forgiveness of him and it was difficult to uphold! The family once more blew apart and this time too, she blamed herself for not being a good enough mother to soothe their souls and so did they!

She threw herself back into her life mission but this time there was a collapse in her own view of the world and she realized that these so called "civilized" humans are not all they are cracked up to be! Then disaster struck again and she was unceremoniously booted off of her mission and had to begin again. Could she do it? Could she survive outside of the system again? She had started making an affirmation and writing it down as a password for a reunion with her tribe and hopefully her children. She discovered that her writing was powerful and every time she wrote about something it seemed to happen.

She even remembered the book she had written as a child about a little girl who ran away to an island. She remembered also a belief that she would never be able to go abroad and her desire to write a book that was blocked by a belief that it probably would never happen. She also remembered a huge desire and statement she had often made about living by the sea.

Out of the blue she decided to uproot totally and used her redundancy money to pay for a rented house on an island. She also decided to go abroad to Turkey and visit a friend who had been a much needed source of spiritual support throughout her journey. She had conquered two massive blocks in her life that she thought she could never achieve and it had all happened in less than a year. Her affirmation for reunion started to come true too, most of her children started to visit her and one of them was forced to live with her for a while by circumstances beyond their control. It was of course an uneasy peace and the saying "be careful of what you wish for because it might come true" started ringing in her ears.

She still believed that the book was out of the question though!

Sitting alone in her new house beside the sea, she contemplated this creation. Sure she had moved to the sea, it was just a stone's throw away, she had a lovely big house but she had not visited the sea once. She had been abroad and expanded her horizons and she had managed to bust blocks. But she was also finding it very hard to get work and the work she had found was not quite paying off yet. She now sat contemplating her fate as her children still continued to have issues with each other and she was still getting attacked by some of them.

Something stirred inside of her and she remembered things that had been said to her by people about book writing. She had started a couple of times but the concept became so big that she would have ended up writing for years and never finishing and so she abandoned it each time. One person said "people haven't got time nowadays to read big books". Another person she knew had just written a book and many people were telling her she should too. She just couldn't work out how to get everything she had to say into a little book that people would be bothered to read. Then it hit her! She doesn't have to write it all, she can just write little books about different things. Small projects are much easier to handle and so in her boredom and fear of the future she wrote a book! Just like that! It took her about 3 days and it was done!

"There"! She said; "That's it I am done, I can die quite happily now knowing that I have accomplished all three desires". But then thought; "So what was the point in all of that if everything I have discovered dies with me? My children don't really know much about me, they still see me through the eyes of their father. I know it has changed a bit but they still sometimes think I am trying to hurt them and start attacking me, so I can't really get the point across to them. So what comes next"?

Then she noticed that the people around her that had read her book started to speak to her about a reflection of the journey she had written about in their own lives in the same way i.e. as she wrote it she experienced huge examples happening in her own life and on the planet and so did they as they read it. A bit like the film "Jumanji". She noticed that it played out her life with more prominence as she wrote and she was clearly able to see her own blocks and understand herself more just like they were as they read. She was shown once again that you need not be afraid of the dark. She had worried that her views on the world would be seen as dark, she knew this wasn't the case and she had learned over her time as an adult that the dark is not something to be afraid of. In fact it is necessary to go into the dark to shine a light on what has been forgotten. She knew that monsters are at their most scary in the dark or when we are asleep in our dreams. When we wake up or shine a light they dissolve or can be faced.

She started to write another book, driven by synchronicity and circumstances. She started to wonder if the book was writing her fate or if she was creating these things to happen. She noticed that loved ones were acting roles in the things she was writing about and she became very aware that whilst writing the darkest chapters in her book her own life was a reflection and so was the planet. She spoke to her dearest fairy friend Nikki about it and she said; "best get on to creating the great stuff parts then eh"? They both giggled at the idea of this magic ☺

That night she was visited by her "higher self" and was given the right questions to enable her to put together the meanings of her life, to create the tree from the split logs.

Her higher self was quite a mischievous older woman, portly and welcoming with a "no nonsense approach". "How you doing Mand"? she said with a look that showed she knew it was crap and Mandy was in a pickle. "Oh, I don't know", said Mandy; "My life is in great upheaval. I am balanced between this great potential for the future and the darkness of the abyss of nothing else"! "Oh dear" said her higher self, "You can't feel your connection to source, you think you are making it all up about your potential future and the darkness is the only thing that is real"? "Yes, spot on" said Mandy "I get stuck when I try to find me nowadays. There was a time in my life when I was much more sure of who I am in my fantasy and possible past life stuff and it gave me a connection to how my life was playing out with much more meaning. But I think I might probably have got a bit too carried away because my path shows that I am not invincible and so therefore can choose the wrong path. I think I am on that wrong path now". "Excuse me for being confused" said Willow (The name Mandy called her higher self), "but I thought we agreed that there was no such thing as a wrong path"? "Oh f*ck off with your 'all is well' slant" said Mandy by this time getting a bit hopeless around the prospect of ever finding anybody to understand! "Look, I am getting very exhausted when it comes to keep restarting from scratch and my children are lost when it comes to understanding what is important for me. True, some of them are helping me to survive this desert I find myself in, but I often also am finding myself at the 'butt end' of their past assumptions about me. I often blame their father's influence for teaching them it is ok to speak to me disrespectfully. But I also blame myself for listening to them and believing they knew the way. Even when they were little, I rarely put rules on them other than to make sure it looked like they were following his. I often let them make choices about what we should do when he wasn't around and even remember sometimes believing they knew a better way than I did. I put that down to my Father bossing me around too much, I just can't seem to change it". "So what about remembering the origins instead of trying to change it" said Willow by this time realizing where Mandy had become blocked. "I do understand it" said Mandy; "I just told you the origins and I know about all the subconscious stuff attached. I explored myself for years remember"? "Yes I know" said Willow, but you stopped at your birth" "No I didn't"! Said Mandy, "I even investigated epigenetics, I know about the impacts of the womb and the mother's perception. I know about the impacts of the genetic cultural inheritance, I know the "who was I" and "how do I fit in the cultures of the past" that valued the woman stuff but I just don't really know if it is true"? "Yes" said Willow, "you know it intellectually; you picked that up from the "stinkers". Remembering means joining with it not just knowing about it. Remember the stuff you know about the ancient cultures, remember the fact that children were seen as messengers of the new knowledge? Your belief was not caused by your father or any other persons experience but in your own experiences of being there when it happened. That's why you act on it, it's because you feel It, It is not just an intellectual concept it is a memory. Nobody is to blame for your actions today, except your own experiences". "Yea I know what you mean, it does seem like a left over from children as the messengers of the new knowledge" said Mandy "but I do, do that sometimes when I am considering past lives, I haven't forgotten about it, I know I have a way to go before I truly believe it. It just doesn't seem like a very important thing to think about when you are trying to survive in a war zone"! Willow had hit her target; "It is the most important thing, this is a time when your memories that emerge can put the logs back together to reveal the tree, this is when you go further in finding out who you are. Remember the journey of the master is one of up's and down's, the straight path means little and creates no hero's journey. These times are abundant and ripe with meaning and the ground is just being prepared for planting the seeds of a new way. The soil has just been dug up and has uncovered the stuff that needs to mulch down and dissolve back from whence it came. Consider the power of the pen, consider your own experiences and what has been uncovered lately. The magic is beginning to work again, your love for humanity is beginning to blossom once more. The fact that you were so sure you would never go abroad, your dancing and singing when you escaped your captor, your desire to be near the sea. What about your fear of talking about your spiritual beliefs because of judgment from society? You knew it was irrational because you could talk about your alcoholism and other drug fuelled escapades with no fear whatsoever. You were not judging society as it is, you were remembering a time when you were tortured and burnt. What about your fear of wrinkles that is starting to develop as you are being largely ignored by the general public". "Oh man; yes" said Mandy, I am getting dismissed by people all over the place and they don't even know they are doing it. A very different reaction to the ones I get when I cover my wrinkles somewhat with makeup or when I was younger". But I remember a time when you were younger" teased Willow, "when you used to look at older women with wrinkles and wish you had some". "Yea but that was only because the father of my children kept going off and having affairs with older women" retorted Mandy. "Sort it out"! said Willow, "you are not as dim as that! These people that you responded to in this life, who helped set the patterns, were there at your request to bring this into your awareness at this point in your life, they are not the cause they are the reminder. Wake up and remember who you are, you are a pen bearer and story teller from Alma Diosa! Did you not see the significance of moving to a house by the sea in a road called 'Alma' where you busted your blocks? You drew on a memory from the sea and you faced your block of never going abroad and you wrote a book"! "Yea but i haven't visited the sea and my book is not a best seller. What's the point of a book that can work magic if it sits on the shelf unread"? Said Mandy. "Tut! You really are lost in this crap aren't you" stated Willow. "The pen bearers craft speaks to the universe and doesn't need to be read! You are speaking to the source of creation and those that read it will have their own memories stirred by it yes, but their journey is their own and if they have found your book then they were meant to because they can understand it consciously! They make those changes and create their futures in their own power! And as for not having visited the sea; you are close to the ocean's source of energy creation and you know you are connected to everything through water; a few bricks and a short walk does not stop the energy zapping you".

"Well, I really like your idea of me being a special one and all that, I just don't feel very special at the moment" laughed Mandy. "Bloody hell"! said Willow whilst raising her left eyebrow; "Do I have to spell everything out to you? Every soul is special, the new ones who know nothing about this planet are special, the middle age souls and the old souls who have been here for years playing the aggressor are too. Think about the task they took on, you have often spoken about this, they could say they were more special than the pen bearers of peace even using your measure and the fact that you don't feel more special than anybody else is the very thing that makes you worthy of the magic. Is one piece of the jigsaw more special than any other?

Can we start piecing it together now without your goddamned ego getting in the way"?

"Of course" replied Mandy rather sheepishly, I was thinking about the 'Chinga connection'. I was talking to a new found friend who is a female Shaman from Peru, about discovering that my nickname meant "f**k" in Spanish, when she told me the longer meaning of "Chingada" I have lived my whole life as a woman who allows herself to be raped! We all have if you think about the rape of the feminine energy and the ghosts of ourselves we have become. It also makes sense as a memory if I was burned at the stake as a witch to have feared talking about my spiritual beliefs". Willow thought for a moment and asked Mandy about any comforting words that she might remember from her childhood. "Yes you know there are many" said Mandy "but one that does stick in my mind is Konkchiel, it meant nothing at the time"! "Other than sounding similar to Konkachila" said Willow, "The Alma Diosan's word for Grandfather of the sky". "Yea I can see that connection" said Mandy, but why not Kuhkoomtheyna meaning grandmother, why Grandfather"? "You needed to retain your connection to a masculine force whilst learning how to fight and be strong enough to deal with what lay ahead" Willow whispered as she watched Mandy put it all together. The running away to the Island of horses writing thing, the connection to the wizard and not the witch, the addiction to giving gifts, the born outside of tribe idea, even the "keep going back for more" thing".

On reading Mandy's thoughts, Willow breathed; "Yes Mandy" that came from the past lives where you kept reincarnating to try to turn the tide. This damaged you in some ways because you saw your culture change over a few hundred years and you got confused and didn't know how to be; so you turned to artificial transcendence and fell into forgetfulness. Your love for the human race was borne as a pain and your magic stopped creating and turned to destruction. You realized that the next step if you came back to the Island was to become part of the aggressor energy in your next creation, you know; the so called "darkness bearers", to fight for freedom in wars that added to the strife already on the planet. You decided to take time out and await the birth of the new souls; you knew you had to learn patience. Did you not wonder why patience had been such an important lesson for you in this life? "Yes, yes, of course" said Mandy, I learned this lifetime that I had to wait for the right moment and not get into things too quickly because I carry a deconstruction energy that breaks down barriers. If rush forward too quickly or rather, too naively, this can create havoc"!

So Mandy finally got it! There is nothing particularly special about any of us unless we are as special as each other. Her lifetime on this planet reflects her journey in previous lives, we are on a never ending journey and all we have to do is find ourselves and remember our mother!

We leave her now finding the many more connections that have come up along her journey like; fitting so easily into any culture and her ease at living in ways connected to the earth. The destruction of her dancing and singing years that did not take into account the impact on others and ultimately herself as she focused on her own needs as an individual rather than as a part of a family. The huge fear she had of losing her loved ones, the dream of running away from the witch and her need to face up to wisdom and being a woman; and not run away from it that is symbolized within the dream. The dark holds nothing that can hurt you if you shine a light on it and neither do witches. The journey is about the richness of the dark fertile soil and the promise that the new shoots deliver. The beautiful bloom that appears when those shoots are nurtured and illuminated and the poignancy when the flower dies and creates the new seeds of abundance that hold the mystery of the future.

Mandy had decided to talk to her friend Anne-Marie, in Turkey, to help bring this magic back into alignment. She is a very talented tarot reader, this friend who she is sure could be an incarnated angel. Anne-Marie drew the cards and told her that she needed to make affirmations to attract some abundance and she said; "writing it down was more powerful". She had just had a huge experience with it herself and was passing on the creation energy. Mandy had not said anything at this point about the chapter in the book she was on and as she was just finishing off her rewritten script this was such a significant message it just had to be from spirit.

Her long term struggle with abundance had come from her lack of desire to compete or follow rules and so she had often failed to push herself forward in the queue. Sure; her father had been the reminder but he was not the cause. She now felt the cause as a connection to a time when the rape of the resources had left little for the native population. Where the covetous nature of the stinkers had shown her the death and destruction that comes with being addicted to possessions and her real struggle to define herself as this became mainstream and she did not want to be like them. She felt the fear of losing her love that had sparked a nomadic lifestyle for her and her people. She remembered the demise of the gift giving and had split; giving and receiving into good and bad. She remembered that she had to be very one-sided to show that she was different, because when she celebrated receiving she had been branded by the "stinkers" as greedy and grasping in their weapons of propaganda. She had internalized the imbalance. Realizing that the flow of "gifts" also depends on receiving for balance, she finally "got it", that she was representing an imbalance and would always get wiped out by the natural laws if she did not rectify this.

"Right" I hear her say as I disappear into the magical place of the observer:

"Universal creators; Konkachila and Kuhkoomtheyna, I am doing everything I can to add my piece of the jigsaw, and remember who I am without letting my ego block me for the good of humanity. I just think it is time for me to receive help now too and I am asking for abundance and nurturance for my soul and my humanness to ease my path. The comfort that is mine by right of being born on this abundant planet and reflects the natural balance; on this, the next stage of my journey. Thank you"!

And so she wrote it into her new script...

13 RED FOR GO!

Well! I think I am done; this book has given me a lot to think about and I hope you have enjoyed it as much as I have. The whole planet appears to be in transition at the moment and we have some serious choices to make in lots of different areas and on lots of different levels. The main things that have been reinforced for me is the importance of valuing diversity, uncovering our connections to a deeper intelligence through studying the past and who we are, and recognizing that we are all a part of keeping this system alive in some ways. Finding ourselves is absolutely vital to creating great relationships with our human family, it allows us to stop pointing fingers of blame and take responsibility for ourselves instead of joining in and playing the roles that create the cult of oppression and hierarchy.

One of the main things that gets in the way of this is our inability to listen without making assumptions. My own experiences when I developed my active listening ability during my early years at college really opened my eyes and supported an ability to get to the heart of the matter. For instance, I had been "snubbed" on many occasions by a young woman who was taking the same course as me. I had tried to talk to her a few times because I liked her. I decided that she must be a bit of a snob and left it at that and considered my own attractions and projections. Then one session called for us to give each other feedback and I had seen her belittle herself earlier on. I told her that she seems to be acting on a belief in her own inadequacy. She lowered her eyes and walked away. The next week she came bounding up to me at the start of the session and said: "Thank you so much! You helped open my eyes to what I have been doing to myself. I felt totally inadequate around you, you know so much and I really admire your honesty and your knowledge. I just felt like I couldn't possibly have a conversation with you because I would make myself look stupid". She wasn't being a snob; she was actually putting me on a pedestal! If I had acted on my belief that she didn't like me, in a hurt way, she might not have liked me quite so much ☺ I might have told others about her rudeness and how she was causing me pain. She would probably be even more damaged by any consequences of me showing dislike, she then might have said things about me that were damaging too!

Another amusing example happened whilst I was waiting in line for the printer at work. Another teacher/manager was often there at the same time and we used to spark up conversations about the lunacy of the management team meetings we both had to attend. Every time I said something about it, he used to respond with "Oh come on" then add his bit. It really confused me, I couldn't work out if he was a friend or foe. His energy felt alright but this phrase in my culture means; "you are talking a load of cr*p"! Because English is his second language I decided to find out what it meant to him. When I asked him the next time he said it, he replied; "I don't know, it doesn't mean anything, it's just something I hear said before English people speak back to each other". When I told him its meaning where I come from, we both laughed and he said; "no wonder people keep getting the hump with me when I talk to them, I thought they were just a bunch of a**holes" ☺

We judge each other based on our own projections of past experiences and "silly stuff" starts to happen when we don't clarify. You know; Like the stuff that happened in the Americas, like the stuff that still happens globally, like the way we interpret the past through patriarchal lenses.

There is another way to discover and create; by adding direct knowing not just conceptual knowledge. There is a huge difference, a bit like tasting the honey and not just being able to describe it. These are two different forms of expansion in my opinion. If somebody asks you to explain honey and you use your left brained masculine skills of exploring the chemical makeup, investigating the bee's themselves and how it is produced etc and how they live from a patriarchal view-point, but have never seen or tasted honey, this is a form of knowing related to thinking about what others say and you could explain very well with lots of words. But this would be from others knowledge and your own cultural conditioning too.

Through patriarchal lenses, our honey bees might be living in an evil matriarchy with an oppressive mother who kills her mates through the act of sex and uses her people as slaves. This is conceptual knowledge. On the other hand, the person who eats the honey but has not investigated the concepts of the bee hive through somebody else's translation but had tended them, could explain through direct knowing, their experience of honey, possibly using feminine based right brain skills... i.e. what did it taste like? Did I like it? What did it feel like? This would be a very subjective experience and if asked what they knew about honey, they would probably not have much to say about it. They might also be able to feel the sense of Matriarchy i.e. the Mother as the creator and the servant of the people; the drones are the only males and live just for procreation, ("Mmmm... Interesting comparison here") and the workers are being rewarded for their 21 day service to the good of the hive, all are female and get the great experiences of tasting the nectar and gathering the honey of life... Neither one of these types of knowing has the whole picture, a bit like the masculine feminine divide; we need both in partnership and both living in harmony and equality to recreate the balance. So I am nowadays exploring the concepts of what others have said about different viewpoints and putting it together in relation to myself and my own experiences to be able to consider the truth from both sides... Interestingly enough my dragons head' (north node of the moon on the day of my birth "*Caput Draconis*") is in Libra, balance!

Another thing I witnessed during my early years of teaching and counseling was that people often told others what particular things symbolize and helped the other person analyze what it was showing in them from a one sided perspective. For instance during a creative session where students were asked to draw a house that represented them, an Asian woman drew a beautifully colorful house with flowers everywhere and lots of decoration. In the windows she had painted red curtains. "There, you see" said one of the tutors; "she is angry and it is the window to her soul, I knew she was not all she claimed"! This was an appalling lack of awareness of cultural diversity. Red means lots of different things in different cultures but in Asia it largely means happiness and prosperity. Imagine the difficulties that could come from the differences in meaning here unless the student was asked to define it, that tutor would form an opinion. The tutor might well say; "I won't let my knowledge of her hidden anger, color my beliefs about her" but this same tutor also told me that I must leave any transference outside the door of the counseling room. So this student may well have found herself kicked off of the course for not displaying enough self awareness as the tutor projected her own stuff onto her, she did in fact seethe with unrecognized anger herself at times. Transference is a tool in counseling, it is our intuition and connection to the client. We must be able to know ourselves in an ever deepening way, to do this we must learn about ourselves when we are with clients and not sit there analyzing them from our own perspective. We need to do this with the rest of humanity too, and then we might be able to work it out.

A thing that is often overlooked is that a coin has two sides. Often we see symbols, gestures, practices and behaviors as having single meanings and so therefore put them in boxes which does not enable us to resolve complex problems or see the bigger picture. A good example of these differences is found in people who hold the power and those that don't. There is an interesting film on youtube that is entitled "[xxxiii]Was Jimmy Savile a Wizard". The film names him as a 7th son, born with magic powers and he often used hand gestures and symbols to mesmerize and call on the powers of the occult. He wore a robe with an 11 pointed star of Thelema; Aleister Crowley's religion that states "Do as though wilt shall be the whole of the law". He used jingles and spoke in "three's" He understood sexual magic and the balance of opposites. By all accounts his dark side was of such depravity that the details are difficult to hear. Yet his charity work was a phenomenal success. He was born on Halloween which is a time when the door to the other world is opened and the souls of the ancestors can come into our world. These are all beliefs and symbols connected to the goddess cultures of magic and balance. As a result, people who do not understand, that wisdom is the ability to hold contradictory ideas and still be ok with each of them would need to chose one or the other meanings and probably argue with each other about who is right. You see, the hand symbols are often used by natural 'witches', they have many different meanings yet I am noticing people pointing out hand gestures used by celebrities as meaning they were part of a satanic cult. They may well be, but they may well be using the magic to effect peace, we cannot tell without exploring their beliefs and intent with them. We are seeing a frenzy of confusion and finger pointing. We are seeing people who are largely trying to uncover corruption being accused of being a "shill" (dis-information merchant) and with sometimes very little evidence. One of the big shocks of our time was the uncovering of Rolf Harris, he was "everybody's favorite grandfather figure" and this has resulted in people not knowing who to trust! There are many so called good and bad people in every profession and in every level of life, if we start to panic and use our egos to prove we are right we are just going to keep this patriarchal system alive and many injustices could occur. We need a dialogue and we all need to develop our listening and empathy skills instead of fighting each other, and trying to analyze people connected to the boxes; we might then just start to come up with solutions.

Whilst there is a contradiction between the need to let go of the past and remembering the past, we also need to understand that "letting go of the past" does not mean forgetting it; it just means dealing with our own sh*t in that. Neither does remembering the past mean we bring it up and throw it in people's faces as blame, we need to deal with our own sh*t in that too. You see it all comes down to changing ourselves and not trying to change others but to understand them.

The Jimmy Savile thing is a prime example of confusion

in what is good and what is bad. One of his trademarks was the "jim'll fix it" tag. This was a program where children's dreams were made to come true and Jimmy Savile was the benevolent provider. He certainly also represented the satanic culture of child abuse and absolute power! He was an enlightened one and one of his sayings was very telling:

""I am like a sewing machine needle that goes in here and goes in there, but I am also the eminence grise: the grey, shadowy figure in the background. The thing about me is I get things done and I work under cover."

The thing with secret societies like Thelema and masonry is that the members are largely isolated in their order and usually only know what the one above and the one below are saying. This sewing machine needle was the holder of all different areas of knowledge that allowed him to operate successfully within the web. He was a Knight of Malta and a Knight of the realm. He hobnobbed with many rich and famous people including politicians and celebrities. He was even asked to mentor Charles and Diana during their separation. He also worked with the sick, the dysfunctional and the poor, whilst also being well involved with those people who helped these "poor unfortunate souls". This gave him access to areas of knowledge that were not known to most of the others. When he died so it all came out! He was the sewing needle that began the process of joining the dots and bringing this institutional abuse to light.

Jim'll fix it? He certainly fixed that one didn't he!

You see all is only able to be labeled as good or bad if you stop at a certain point. Yes bad things happened as they do in life generally, but they brought public enlightenment. We need to remember the journey of the master and the fact that disasters always bring better times in a never ending journey of highs and lows.

Forgiveness and sanity is also needed here, how can somebody confess or throw light on anything if they are going to get attacked if they do? Surely we do not want this new way to be birthed in the blood of the guilty do we? It is up to us to create the nurturing environment that we need to learn humanity's lessons and that means all of us are important and as we all carry some guilt, where do we draw the line?
My final thought for this book is of questioning everything and that doesn't mean rejecting stuff but finding the deeper knowledge.

The number 13 has always been understood by me as being unlucky as I am sure most people understand it that way too. You may also have noticed that there are 13 chapters in each of my books? This is because I have discovered that the number 13 was linked to witches and covens and so therefore needed further examination. But also the first question I ever answered correctly at school was "how many buns in a baker's dozen"? The answer is of course 13 but as it had stuck in my mind as a childhood memory, I decided to uncover the truth. There are 13 moons in a year and 13 fertility cycles in women. This number is linked to nature and the magic of women and witches. All of the other female archetypes are about the "man box" you know; virgin or queen or mother whilst the witch was cast out and became a forbidden form of feminine magic. 13 breaks down to 4 in numerology and so symbolizes the stages of metamorphosis.

Witches or wizards can symbolize magic and women have been branded as possessing evil magic for far too long, while the male magic that is responsible for where we are today in this cesspit of human disconnect is not spoken of and resides in secret places. I feel that as it is time for change and my intent is of joining together in harmony rather than dividing for control and power I can share my knowledge and access this magic in positive ways. As magic is really just about symbolism and our beliefs are all guided by symbols, then my intent will create harmonic magic with the help of 13; or so the theory goes.

On a final note; I referred to Sarah-Jane Grace the spiritual astrologer at the beginning of this book and would like to self indulge here and finish off this book with an excerpt from one of her astrology readings on me that really helped me to understand myself and get into my magic:

Chiron in Aquarius in 3rd House

"Your healing gift is extremely hard to put into words for you dance with the Universal flow in order to translate the seemingly untranslatable and to make the unknowable known. You have a connection to the past, present and future that enables you to actively work with layers of consciousness in order to bring new understandings and wisdom. This can relate specifically to past events in history but also to personal evolution as well for you dance with great beauty and grace enabling you to connect freely with Truth. You are a Bodhisattva (wisdom being) and your compassion radiates out far and wide in the world. Your desire to heal comes from a compelling inner need to make a positive difference and to make your own pain and suffering worthwhile through wisdom, learning, evolution and growth. You dance and weave a web of creativity, inspiration, love, compassion and empowerment. As a Bodhisattva, you are an enlightened soul and others seem drawn to you as your aura of compassion and understanding radiates like a lighthouse. You see beyond perception and human boundaries, touching the lives of so many. And yet, despite your ability to have such an impact, your own missing link continues in earnest as you try to find peace within and in your life; you are seeking a sense of acceptance within your Self that brings you a feeling of finally being home".

I really resonated with this idea and looked further into what "bodhisattva" meant:

The word *bodhisattva* means "enlightenment being." Very simply, bodhisattvas are beings who work for the enlightenment of all beings, not just themselves. They vow not to enter Nirvana until all beings enter Nirvana together.

I looked further and discovered that this type of energy involves "getting over yourself" not trying to be perfect! Imperfection is where we are all at and we might as well admit it, otherwise people will feel inadequate in our presence...

Just one last request I rather fancy entering Nirvana, so can we all get on with it please? ☺

ABOUT THE AUTHOR

Mandy is a teacher of counseling, psychology and sociology as well as a practicing counselor. She has trodden the experiential path as well as the theoretical and abstract. She holds a bachelor of arts degree in integrative counseling and a PCE in teaching. Her journey towards "enlightenment" started some 18 years ago, when she finally escaped from a 20 year abusive relationship. Then, after 4 years of alcohol and other drug abuse, she emerged to face up to a spiritual path that she had denied existed. Her descent into hell has given her many examples to draw upon as she questions the conditioned view of the world and offers a different perspective.

When asked if she is a feminist, she often replies:

I remember when I told my counselor about my journey and value system, he said "So you are a feminist then" I nearly choked! No I ain't I loudly proclaimed! I am a humanist! However, because this title has already been taken over by a patriarchal theoretical concept, He was more right than me!

There is nothing wrong with calling something by its differences, at the moment we need to, to show the divide and feminism in my book now supports the mother principle and we need to give it as much public acclaim as patriarchy once had... Just to balance the sides. Then of course we can collectively call it something we all agree on. I do agree very much with your observation of this creating problems but I think it's more a problem with the group than the word.

She has many years of experience, leading groups of people from a multitude of diverse cultures from across the planet, on a journey towards togetherness and now shares some of her wisdom in this book.

[i] Sarah-Jane Grace http://www.sarahjanegrace.com/
[ii] Andrew Norton-Webber http://aquariusthewaterbearer.com/
[iii] Bruce Lipton https://www.brucelipton.com/about
[iv] Freudian slip This word just came out as I was writing and is not my usual expression http://www.dailymail.co.uk/sciencetech/article-2161115/Theory-Freudian-slip-confirmed-experiments-new-research-claims.html
[v] The secret http://www.amazon.com/The-Secret-Rhonda-Byrne/dp/1582701709
[vi] Capitalist ideology http://www.quick-facts.co.uk/politics/ideologies.html
[vii] Freedom programme http://www.freedomprogramme.co.uk/
[viii] Power and control wheel

(www.theduluthmodel.org/wheelgallery.php).

"Making the Power and Control Wheel gender neutral would hide the power imbalances in relationships between men and women that reflect power imbalances in society. By naming the power differences, we can more clearly provide advocacy and support for victims, accountability and opportunities for change for offenders, and system and societal changes that end violence against women".

Fuctifino!

POWER AND CONTROL

PHYSICAL VIOLENCE SEXUAL

USING COERCION AND THREATS
Making and/or carrying out threats to do something to hurt her • threatening to leave her, to commit suicide, to report her to welfare • making her drop charges • making her do illegal things.

USING INTIMIDATION
Making her afraid by using looks, actions, gestures • smashing things • destroying her property • abusing pets • displaying weapons.

USING EMOTIONAL ABUSE
Putting her down • making her feel bad about herself • calling her names • making her think she's crazy • playing mind games • humiliating her • making her feel guilty

USING ISOLATION
Controlling what she does, who she sees and talks to, what she reads, where she goes • limiting her outside involvement • using jealousy to justify actions.

MINIMIZING, DENYING AND BLAMING
Making light of the abuse and not taking her concerns about it seriously • saying the abuse didn't happen • shifting responsibility for abusive behavior • saying she caused it.

USING CHILDREN
Making her feel guilty about the children • using the children to relay messages • using visitation to harass her • threatening to take the children away.

USING MALE PRIVILEGE
Treating her like a servant • making all the big decisions • acting like the "master of the castle" • being the one to define men's and women's roles

USING ECONOMIC ABUSE
Preventing her from getting or keeping a job • making her ask for money • giving her an allowance • taking her money • not letting her know about or have access to family income.

PHYSICAL VIOLENCE SEXUAL

DOMESTIC ABUSE INTERVENTION PROJECT
202 East Superior Street
Duluth, Minnesota 55802
218-722-2781
www.duluth-model.org

[ix] UBUNTU http://www.harisingh.com/UbuntuAge.htm
[x] David E Stannard "The American holocaust
https://www.youtube.com/watch?v=ju1ag1geRnM

[xi] The Spanish Requerimiento was a "requirement" (A demand) and a written declaration of sovereignty and war. This was read by Spanish military forces to assert their sovereignty (control) over the Americas.

[xii] How America is like a bad boyfriend
https://www.youtube.com/watch?v=K8flfOeWMPQ&feature=share

[xiii] **MENTAL HEALTH CASE STUDY**

Afro Caribbean male age 38.

Was brought to the hospital after being arrested by the police for violent disturbance. He had been behaving in a highly sensitised and agitated manner whilst in his cell. It was also mentioned that he had been acting and making noises like an animal and showed no relational understanding to people around him.

Setting: Hospital in-patient under section

Preparedness: unable to ascertain (client confusion)

Connections: alone in a foreign country

Emotional state: under mild sedation, became agitated, does not know the difference between real and unreal/dead or alive.

Action plan: not suitable for counselling. Referral to psychiatrist re signs of schizophrenia/psychosis.

Client recently moved to this country (18 months ago) is unemployed and lives in social isolation. There is a history of cannabis use and violent incidents. He was sectioned under the mental health act after a violent attack on the police. He spoke of white people in authority with hatred and jealousy i.e. "they should all be murdered, why should they have a nice life when I am dead". He lives in social isolation making no efforts to integrate into the community. He has hallucinations of being surrounded in light and a belief that he is talking to god. He states that police/social workers/medical staff are following him and use violence against him.

States that police "murdered him when he came to this country"

M: how did they murder you?

A: they cut my heart out

M: they cut your heart out?

A: yes then they buried me in a grave

M: how come you are here?

A: I'm not really

M: where are you then?

A: I told you I'm dead and buried in my grave (agitated gestures)

M. how come I can see you?

A: you can't see me I'm invisible no one can see me you think you can but you can't

M: why would I say I could if I can't?

A: because you are like the rest of them mad white men, they all think they can see but they can't really they are all mad. You are mad you just think you're not.

(Groaned, you're all mad throwing his arms around and smiling at the same time)

M: you seem very angry

A: I'm not angry, I told you, you can't see me. Don't keep telling me I'm angry, everyone says that but how can they say that if they cant see me. No one can see me.

Client started to wave his arms around angrily and his face contorted in anger. At this point I felt very threatened and pushed the panic button.

The client was restrained and removed shouting angrily that everyone was mad.

Client seems to be exhibiting delusional behaviour in that he believes the police murdered him and he is buried in a grave. He shows signs of psychotic disorder, possibly cannabis induced.

His ability to differentiate between real and unreal shows signs of impairment through his belief that he is invisible and dead. Fernando (1996)

There are some pointers towards paranoid schizophrenia with persecutory/grandiose delusions, themed with jealousy and anger. The fact that he has been involved in violent incidents consistently with authority figures is another warning sign towards paranoid schizophrenia. There also appears to be incongruity in his behaviour such as smiling as he throws his arms about in angry gestures. From the limited information gained from the client it seems that there has been a rapid deterioration of his personality within the past year i.e. "I used to be happy now I hate everyone". American psychiatric association (2005)

I would deem this client unsuitable for counselling in view of the above symptoms and the way forward appears to be referral to a psychiatrist antipsychotic drugs and possible electroplexy.

CLIENTS STORY
I came to this country 18 months ago. When I first came here I was happy and carefree. I was excited about the new life I dreamed of and the new people I was going to meet. My family was going to follow later, but I am now scared for them if they come to this country.

I tried to get work and found it difficult to get a job. I was sworn at and called names by people. I was told to fuck off home and my home had eggs thrown at the windows. I had bad words painted on my walls. And I was frightened to go out.

I was walking home after an unsuccessful search for a job and the police stopped me. They said they wanted to search me and I didn't know why. I started to tell them how hard it was to be accepted in this country and they became edgy, they told me to calm down and it made me frustrated because they were not listening to me. They knocked me to the floor and handcuffed me. Whilst I was on the floor they sprayed my eyes with cs gas and it made me angry. I began to struggle because I was scared. They hit me with their truncheons and took me to the cells. Later they took me to the hospital for an x-ray. When we went in the police spoke to the medical staff. The staff became agitated and I tried to explain to them that I wasn't angry. I was restrained again and later taken to court. I was sent to prison. When I came out I kept getting stopped by the police and some times arrested. I am called names and attacked everywhere I go. I got a job in a factory and was not accepted by people. I was searched at the gate one night and they found property belonging to work in my pockets. I didn't know how it had got there. Then I saw some people from work watching and laughing. I think they put it there. I shouted for them to tell them what they had done and the police were called. They didn't give me a chance to talk; they just restrained me and took me to the cells.

I am a shaman and practice awakening of kundalini. I put myself in this aroused state to help me survive the experience of this country. I am aware of my physical symptoms whilst in this state. I some times laugh or cry, I talk in tongues, I sometimes go limp or rigid and I make animal-like movements and sounds. Before the mystical experience occurs I am very sensitive to everything around me, I have strong emotional reactions and feelings of inadequacy and cannot relate to others around me. (See appendix)

The police did not understand me and they sent a medical doctor. I was put into this hospital; I have been drugged and tied up. They act like I am dangerous and they keep me locked up.

I have not spoken the language for long and people don't always understand what I am saying, so I try to explain with movements.

When I came to this country I was happy and carefree. The police have murdered me; I used to be alive inside now I am dead. They have opened my chest and ripped out my heart. I am murdered inside and buried under the oppression. When I tell them I have been murdered they tell me I can't be, they say I am still here so I can't be. I don't understand what they mean by that. I can't tell anyone what happened to me I get accused of being angry and dangerous. When I use my arms to show them they grab me and restrain me, they hit me. The drugs have made it difficult to talk, I can't get out of this mess, and I can't get safe anywhere. In hospital I am drugged, in prison I am tied up and in life I am persecuted. All they see is someone angry and violent, they don't see me. I have never hurt anybody in my life. The happy carefree me is buried to these people, they don't see me, nobody sees me.

The person I was speaking to thought I was angry, I was too drugged to explain myself; I thought she was going to help me but she also didn't see me. When I tried to show her what I meant with my arms she became scared, she called the other people and they grabbed me, they dragged me away and they locked me up.

The people in this country are mad.

The psychological perspective in this case is based in lack of cultural understanding, misinterpretation of language; unrecognised racist beliefs i.e. drug crazed violent black men and non-recognition of racial prejudice in this country.

[xiv] A neurosurgeons journey through the afterlife.
https://www.youtube.com/watch?v=qbkgj5J91hE

[xv] Dr Ian Stevenson children's past life memories
https://www.youtube.com/watch?v=Ir9Xs1Q9T5g

[xvi] http://www.thesociologicalcinema.com/videos/the-normalization-of-intimate-partner-violence-in-beauty-and-the-beast

[xvii]

http://www.medicinenet.com/narcissistic_personality_disorder/article.htm

Narcissism
"FRIDAY, Aug. 6 2010 (HealthDay News) -- Ever met a guy who talks only about himself, thinks he's superior to everyone and who tends to view women as little more than playthings? That man may very well have narcissistic personality disorder, a condition marked by an inflated sense of self-importance and a profound lack of empathy for others. And new research suggests the anger, hostility and short fuse that accompany a man's narcissism tend to be directed toward straight women. "Heterosexual, narcissistic men become enraged at people who deny them gratification, whether it's social status, having a trophy partner or sexual gratification," said lead study author Scott Keiller, a clinical psychologist and assistant professor of psychology at Kent State University Tuscarawas in Ohio. "The group that could gratify heterosexual men the

most is heterosexual women," Keiller said. "To the extent narcissistic men would get resistance,that would make them enraged."

For the study, published online July 23 in the journal *Sex Roles*, Keiller and his colleagues gave 104 male undergraduates questionnaires designed to measure narcissism. Questions included: "I love to be the center of attention" or "It embarrasses me when I am the center of attention." The former is associated with narcissism, the latter with modesty and humility. They were also asked about their attitudes toward gay men, lesbians, straight women and other straight men, including how much they ascribed to traditional -- some would say sexist -- male and female stereotypes. None of the men questioned had diagnosable narcissistic personality disorder, said Keiller. (The disorder is diagnosed when one meets five symptoms on a list that includes grandiosity, a strong sense of entitlement, and an overwhelming need for admiration, according to the American Psychiatric Association.) But narcissism is a continuum, and plenty of the young men had a pronounced tendency toward those traits, he said. Men who scored the highest on the narcissism test were more likely to view women as conniving gold diggers, as teases who tempt men with sex and don't deliver, or as seductresses with plans to trick men and "get them under their thumb," Keiller said."Narcissistic men hold overtly hostile, adversarial ideas about women," Keiller said. While narcissistic men also showed rancour toward gay men, their hostility toward them was no worse than that of other straight men. About the only group that escaped narcissistic men's anger were lesbians, possibly because straight men tend to eroticize them, Keiller said. Jean Twenge, a professor of psychology at San Diego State University and author of "The Narcissism Epidemic: Living in the Age of Entitlement," said the study fits with other research on narcissists. "Narcissists don't have a problem with everyone, or with people that are different. They have a problem with people who may reject them," Twenge said. "They have a problem with heterosexual women, because those are the people who might see through them, reject them and not give them the attention and adulation they feel they deserve." The findings suggest they view their relationships with women as patriarchal rather than egalitarian, the authors said. Men tend to have more narcissistic traits than women, possibly because girls, more than boys, are taught to be nurturing, selfless and to put others first, according to background information in the article. Likewise, men are more frequently diagnosed with narcissistic personality disorder than women. Research suggests narcissistic men are also more likely to commit domestic violence because of their egocentrism and lack of empathy, although many men who commit violence are not narcissists, Keiller said".

[xviii] Love and Stockholm syndrome http://drjoecarver.makeswebsites.com/clients/49355/File/love_and_stockholm_syndrome.html
[xix] Free association http://www.simplypsychology.org/psychoanalysis.html
[xx] The history of love and sex
https://www.youtube.com/watch?v=YSZGK7QZHY8
[xxi] Swearing:

http://newsfeed.time.com/2013/04/10/nine-things-you-probably-didnt-know-about-swear-words/
[xxii] Gwynne Dyer
https://www.youtube.com/watch?v=OdaYlSAUr94&feature=youtu.be
[xxiii] Huda Lutfi http://www.aucegypt.edu/fac/Profiles/Pages/HudaLutfi.aspx
[xxiv] http://www.ohio.edu/southern/folknography/upload/Our-Grandmother.pdf
[xxv] http://www.gift-economy.com/articlesAndEssays/principleVsPatriarchal.html
[xxvi] https://www.youtube.com/watch?v=drCzWw14qOA&x-yt-ts=1421914688&x-yt-cl=84503534#t=67
[xxvii] *The Annals*, Boudicca, according to Tacitus, (Written in AD 110-120)
[xxviii] *Dio's Roman History VIII*, By Cassius Dio, a Roman historian (153 AD-230 AD)
[xxix] Five First Pages: Malleus Maleficarum (The witches hammer) by Jacobus Sprenger & Heinrich Kramer
https://www.youtube.com/watch?v=bJXsKg0yVk8
[xxx] Does Brewster Sara deserve a good ducking
http://brewsters.co.uk/category/history/
[xxxi] Edward Bulwer-Lytton
[xxxii] Meaning; Soul goddess.
[xxxiii] Was Jimmy Savile a Wizard" https://www.youtube.com/watch?v=-QUuCWNyvv8

Printed in Great Britain
by Amazon